ON THE INSIDE LOOKING OUT

Renewing Your Mind

Carlton Lee Arnold

On the Inside Looking Out
Renewing Your Mind
by Carlton Lee Arnold

Printed in the United States of America.

ISBN 9781498476584

www.xulonpress.com

To God is ALL the glory!

Being Transformed

And we all,

who with unveiled faces contemplate the Lord's glory,

are being transformed into his image with ever-increasing glory, which comes from the Lord,

who is the Spirit.

2 Corinthians 3:18

A Living Sacrifice

[1]Therefore, I urge you, brothers and sisters, in view of God's mercy, to offer your bodies as a living sacrifice, holy and pleasing to God—this is your true and proper worship.

[2] Do not conform to the pattern of this world, but be transformed by the renewing of your mind. Then you will be able to test and approve what God's will is—his good, pleasing and perfect will.

Romans 12:1-2

Table Of Contents

Introduction

SECTION 3

APPLICATION OF SPIRITUAL TRUTHS TO BECOME CHRIST-LIKE

Introduction

SECTION 4

THE SPIRITUAL CONCEPT OF DEATH

<u>CONCLUSION</u>

Introduction

The purpose of this book is to raise the level of awareness of Believers of the need to spiritually grow to become more Christ-like. The title is to show that spiritual growth in a Christian can only occur as a Believer allows the Holy Spirit inside them to reveal to them who they are from the inside. All of the aspects of becoming more Christ-like must come from allowing God to show us who we are on the inside. Too many Christians assess their spirituality by what they think others see on their outside (actions, attitudes, etc.) A Believer can live their life behind a mask thinking that they will demonstrate spiritual maturity by using only their minds and emotions. It is not how much of the Bible you know, and it is not how you look at a church service from a worship perspective. To become more Christ-like is to give up who you are on the inside and allow the Holy Spirit to direct your life from the inside.

Christianity can be viewed as consisting of two major goals: evangelism and discipleship. Evangelism receives most of the attention of churches, pastors, missionaries, and the regular churchgoer. However, discipleship does not receive as much attention. Both of these activities should be a part of every spiritual growing Christian. This book will focus on the discipleship where you undergo mind changes about your attitudes, behavior, and relationships. Jesus summarized His expectations of all Believers when He said the following just before He ascended to heaven:

> **"Therefore go and make disciples of all nations, baptizing them in the name of the Father and of the Son and of the Holy Spirit, and teaching them to obey everything I have**

> **commanded you. And surely I am with you always, to the very end of the age."** Matthew 28:19-20

The evangelism part of His commands is obvious, but so is the teaching command. The teaching command is usually referred to as discipleship. I want to define discipleship as the renewing of the mind that occurs in Believers to become more Christ-like. In other words, the purpose of this book is to identify areas in your life that may need a change in your mind. Most people will say that this is one of the most difficult things in the world. It is not easy to change people's minds. However, this book strongly recommends that the only true way for a mind-changing event to occur for a Christian is through the power of the Holy Spirit.

If anyone becomes a Christian, the Bible is clear that God expects that person to go through numerous mind-changing events while living their life on earth. This will be the first topic discussed in Section 1. Renewing the mind is a high priority of God for every Believer. Extensive use of Biblical verses will be used to support each point. God intended for every Believer to identify areas in their life that would be considered worldly and not spiritual. After a Believer identifies a worldly behavior (that is usually called sin or flesh), the Bible describes how the mind of Christ should become a part of the Believer.

Section 2 will examine the human being as defined by the Bible. The physical body, the personality, and the spirit of a human being are discussed to establish how a Believer's mindset can be controlled by the world and not by the Spirit. One of the highlights of this section is to examine the soul of Jesus Christ. This book depends heavily upon how the Bible describes the attitudes and actions of Jesus in His relationship with others. Without using the Bible, a Christian will determine their own criteria for being Christ-like, and make it something that they must maintain within themselves. This is why renewing of the mind is necessary for every Christian. This section will help the reader to understand their interaction with the world as compared to the time they spend with God and spiritual things.

Section 3 will discuss 31 specific attributes of a human being that should be exhibited by the Believer as being Christ-like. This section will enable the reader to look in a mirror examining how close their thinking is to that of Christ. It is in this section that Believers will be given the opportunity to see themselves as God sees them and compare that to the way Jesus lived on this earth. They will also grow spiritually deeper in their relationship with God.

Section 4 is a special section on the concept of death. A Believer's concept of death should be the same as that of Christ, and that is spiritual. Most Believers struggle with the concept of death, because death can have such a dramatic impact as viewed worldly. I used numerous Biblical passages to describe death from a spiritual point of view. My sincere wish is that this section not only provides comfort to you if you have lost a loved one, but also will help you live your life on this earth unafraid of the most threatening aspect of living: dying.

It is my hope that when you have finished reading this book, you will make a concerted effort to seek out those events in your life that God is using to alert you to specific mind changes that you must make. Only after Believers demonstrate the mind of Christ through their actions and attitudes can the people in this world see the abundant life that God is offering all Believers.

Section 1

Renewing Your Mind Is A High Priority To God

Introduction

When you were growing as a child and as an adolescent, the major input into your belief system came from the world. What this means is that you put things into your mind that were worldly. You may have had times when God got your attention, but, for the most part, we all learn our values, how to treat others, how to react to adversity, and other issues that define who we are from the things in this world.

Consider the movie, Groundhog Day. Most of the movie is about a character that displays all of the bad sides of a human being. You will see all of the worldly things learned over time by the leading character. However, he learns that if he would deny himself and help others, his life was much more interesting and fulfilled. This is a great redemptive movie where people change from worldliness to Godliness. However, it is not a great evangelistic movie.

As Christians, we all bring worldliness into our lives. Our values may be worldly, and people will have a negative reaction to our behavior. It is this worldliness that God wants to change. The Bible teaches very clearly that, as Christians, God expects us to become more Christ-like. For example, Jesus said in Luke 9:23-25,

Then he said to them all: "Whoever wants to be my disciple must deny themselves and take up their cross daily and follow me. For whoever wants to save their life will lose it, but whoever loses their life for me will save it. What good is it for someone to gain the whole world, and yet lose or forfeit their very self?

These are some tough words spoken by our Lord and Savior. He is basically saying that all Christians should be denying themselves to the point of losing their life. I do not think He is meaning to lose your life by physically dying. He is saying that as you are living in this world, always put others ahead of yourself by considering yourself dead to yourself. This aspect of living is the opposite of the worldly philosophy of putting yourself first, and always trying to be Number One.

In Romans 12:1-2, Paul states the clearest message on renewing your mind:

Therefore, I urge you, brothers and sisters, in view of God's mercy, to offer your bodies as a living sacrifice, holy and pleasing to God—this is your true and proper worship. Do not conform to the pattern of this world, but be transformed by the renewing of your mind. Then you will be able to test and approve what God's will is—his good, pleasing and perfect will.

Similar to the teachings of Jesus, Paul says to offer yourself as a living sacrifice. When you live with that thought in your mind, you will be undergoing mind changes from the world to the kingdom of God. God wants you to live on this earth with the understanding that you will be constantly transforming your mind to be more aligned with the teachings of Jesus. This requires renewing of the mind, and that is what this book is about. The foundation for every discussion is based on Biblical passages.

1. You were created to be like God!

"You were taught, with regard to your former way of life, to put off your old self, which is being corrupted by its deceitful desires; to be made new in the attitude of your minds; and to put on the new self, created to be like God in true righteousness and holiness." Ephesians 4:22-23

These verses talk about a major change that must occur in the life of a Believer. The "old self" is what you would call your selfish ways (it has to be my way; what can I get out of it; why does everything happen to me; no one knows or even cares what I am going through; I need this; I need that). Everything that has to do with self has to be "put off" – removed; eliminated; broken off; not thought about; denied; not to be given into.

The Bible speaks of the "old self" as having a power over you. You can never overcome that power on your own. When you became a Christian, God gave you the Spirit to conquer that "old self". The difference in which one controls your behavior (old self or Spirit) depends on the action you decide to take for any situation. If you decide the old self, then all the power of the flesh consumes you. If you decide the Spirit, then the power that raised Jesus from the dead will flood your soul. Therefore, a Christian must mature in removing the old self within themselves as an influencer of their actions.

And then, you can "put on the new self". You choose to think about God, Christ, others and not your "self". Do you realize how hard that is in today's world? Today's world is all about satisfying "you" (the "old self".) But all the world really wants is your time and money. The world will sap every ounce of energy out of you. You end up empty trying to figure out what is the next thing that will satisfy the "old self". Guess what! Many people have tried everything but have failed.

Solomon (the wisest man who ever lived) conducted several experiments at fulfilling the desires of the flesh. In every experiment, the flesh was never satisfied. You can read the book of Solomon in the Old Testament to learn the details of Solomon's experiments. If you have an addiction to something, you are giving control of your life to something you will never be able to control. This world has nothing that will satisfy the unending need to take care of the "old self".

Only God can satisfy your deepest needs; heal your most painful hurts; and, give you peace that the world will never be able to give you. But, you must "put off the old self" and "put on the new self". When you do, these verses say something that is hard to believe: "created to be like God in true righteousness and holiness." WOW!!! "Like God in true righteousness and holiness". NO WAY!! NOT ME! And, there is the problem...I am thinking of "ME" – the "old self"!

This verse describes the work that God has done to my self without "ME". He has created me as a new creation. I am no longer that old self. HE HAS

CREATED! Do I want to believe God or trust myself to the "old self"? I want to pursue God and forget about this ME stuff, because God thinks a lot about you and me!

2. God thinks a lot about you!

"...you whom I have upheld since you were conceived, and have carried since your birth. Even to your old age and gray hairs I am he, I am he who will sustain you. I have made you and I will carry you; I will sustain you and I will rescue you. Isaiah 46:3b-4

I love these words! God spends more time thinking about you than you do thinking about Him. I think He would like it the other way around. However, we become so easily distracted that we could go for days or weeks and never spend time with God. Read the Bible verses again.

This Bible passage says that God is a very personal God. He is not a God who is somewhere out in space with no concern for this world. God did not set everything up in this world, press a button, and stand back to watch what would happen. This world and you are not an experiment of God's. How do I know? He became flesh Himself and died on a cross for our sins. He became an integral part in the history of humanity regardless of atheists or those who rewrite history. His life has had a permanent and comprehensive impact on the history of human beings. People can doubt Him and not believe in Him, but they cannot deny His impact. He is not a bystander looking on this world with indifference. God is involved in your life on a daily basis!

God became involved in your life when you were conceived! WOW!! This is an amazing truth about God and about you! He personally knows all of the aborted and miscarried babies and takes care of them. Our God is Awesome! He didn't wait for you to get to an age where you could understand Him with your mind. He began taking care of you the moment you were conceived!

It is interesting that, as Believers, we spend more time trying to take care of ourselves without ever acknowledging God's work in our life? It is like what we think and do for ourselves is better than any work that God can do in our lives. Does this make sense? I do not think so. After you were born, God continued to "carry" you. What a comforting thought that the God who made the universe takes the time to "carry" you. When God is carrying you nothing can get to you... you are under His protection. During trials and tragic events in your life, guess who is carrying you? God! Another aspect of "carry" is support. God is providing support for you in your life. And, most of the time, we do not even know it!

God also sustains your life when you are of "old age and gray hairs." This is such an encouraging thought when you reach a point in your life where you lose a spouse and/or your children and grandchildren are too busy to visit you. With only thoughts of yourself, you can easily become lonely and despondent. But, your God says that He will sustain you! He will support you, hold you, provide for you, and help you get through the tough times, and encourage you to endure to the end. No matter how old you are, start spending time with God. Read His Word – the Bible. Pray for your family and others. Meditate on your life and how God is a part of it. Make sure that God is in your life.

3. Believers should think spiritually and not worldly

What is more, I consider everything a loss compared to the surpassing greatness of knowing Christ Jesus my Lord, for whose sake I have lost all things. I consider them rubbish, that I may gain Christ, and be found in him, not having a righteousness of my own that comes from the law, but that which is through faith in Christ – righteousness that comes from God and is by faith. Philippians 3:8-9

The impact of these verses on a Christian is so important to living the abundant life here on earth. God's purpose for your life after becoming a Christian is to change the way you think about things. Instead of worldly thinking, God will bring into your life those events that will cause you to consider things from a spiritual or eternal perspective. This kind of thinking is a huge jolt to many Christians, because of the importance and the priority we have placed on the things of this world.

For example, consider the property that your house sits on. We want to make sure that our neighbors are cutting their grass on time, not putting their garbage cans out too early, keeping up the appearance of the neighborhood, and not painting their house school bus yellow. Why? Our focus is on our property value. We do not want it to decrease but increase. The verses above tell us that Paul would not be worried about those things, because he is thinking of his heavenly home. He is thinking of his eternal life to be lived with God. It does not matter if your neighbor plants some bushes on your property line or even on your property. God would consider your relationship with that neighbor of higher value than those bushes. You can do this only if you consider everything you have and own as rubbish so that you may know Christ. You will be exercising your faith by keeping a healthy relationship with your neighbors so that they will see Christ in you. These thoughts require a renewal of the mind.

Not only do we place an inordinate value on our property, we also place the wrong value on what is inside of our homes. When we purchase carpet and furnishings to make our home look good, we do not want our children, or the neighborhood kids, or our grandchildren to ruin any of our "stuff." We read the "riot act" to our children to keep them from ruining our "stuff." May I suggest that we need to remember that children are like the "Kingdom of God"? It would surprise you how much children can teach us about the things of God if we would give up protecting and worrying over our earthly possessions and spend more time with children.

Also, our righteousness does not come from anything on this earth. This is probably the most abused term for us as Believers. We want to place a self-righteous value based on the things we do or we possess on this earth (like the things discussed above). There is nothing on this earth that will make you righteous. Your most righteous work on this earth should be considered as rubbish. This is what Paul thought about all of his "good deeds." Our righteousness comes from God alone and is given to us freely by the work of Christ on the cross. This should be the focus of our lives, as Believers, on this earth. Others will see the faith you have when you consider everything about you as nothing. It will take faith to "give up" the stock market, your home, your property, and your furnishings. Others will take a second look at you when you do not become upset at losing any value in these earthy items. They will want to know how you do it. This is the eternal purpose that God has for your life: to tell others what Christ has done for you. This cannot be done without a spiritual renewal of the mind.

4. Living a Christian life in an ungodly world

Dear friends, I urge you, as foreigners and exiles, to abstain from sinful desires, which wage war against your soul. Live such good lives among the

pagans that, though they accuse you of doing wrong, they may see your good deeds and glorify God on the day he visits us. 1 Peter 2:11-12

My wife and I have moved numerous times, and each time, we always sought out Christians with whom to have to fellowship. This usually meant finding a church that was true to the gospel of Christ. No matter where we went, we always found strong Christians, weak Christians, questionable Christians, and pagans. It is difficult to label those without Christ in their lives. I am using the word pagans from the verses above. In reality, I never call someone without Christ a certain label. They have been called "lost" which has no meaning to them, because they know where they live. They have been called sinners, but we are all sinners. One possible way is to call them "worldly". This holds true because Christians are, at times, "unworldly".

In the verses above, Peter puts a different perspective on Christians and pagans. He describes Christians as foreigners and exiles (unworldly). I hope this is significant to you. When you accepted Christ, you were separated from this world. Your citizenship changed from the world to the Kingdom of God. You now live in the Kingdom of God and are a stranger to the world. I had to think on this for many years, because I grew up in this world, just like you, and saw and heard and participated in what this world provides. I am now a foreigner to this world. I strongly suggest that you think on this concept to the point that you not only believe it but also understand its ramifications.

Since you and I are no longer citizens of this world, war has been declared on how you live your life. You cannot escape this war. It is a battle between the values of this world and the values of the Kingdom of God. The values of this world are centered on your flesh or your selfish desires. The values of God's Kingdom focus on self-sacrifice and serving others. I hope you can see the significant difference in these two spheres of influence. They share nothing in common. This will be discussed in more detail in Section 2.

While you continue to live in this world, you are not a part of this world. However, the world wages war against your soul. This is why most Christians have a difficult time applying spiritual truths to their lives. It doesn't seem natural to forget about self. Yet, this is why God has given every Christian the Holy Spirit to lead and empower them to live their life guided by the values of God's Kingdom.

When a Christian does live by God's Kingdom, those who are pagans/unbelievers/lost/ ungodly/worldly will see the significance of your self-sacrifice and praise God. I suggest you ask the Holy Spirit to show you the significant difference between the world and God's Kingdom. You can read a newspaper, watch TV or a movie, have a discussion with others, and you will begin to see the huge disparity in living a Godly life and a worldly life.

I think this is an imperative for all Christians. We must be different, because we are strangers to this world. Worldly people need to see the hope that you have in God's Kingdom. It is the only true and solid hope left in this world. This truly requires a renewing of the mind.

5. God used Jesus for you to have a new life

What shall we say, then? Shall we go on sinning so that grace may increase? By no means! We died to sin; how can we live in it any longer? Or don't you know that all of us who were baptized into Christ Jesus were baptized into his death? We were therefore buried with him through baptism into death in order that, just as Christ was raised from the dead through the glory of the Father, we too may live a new life. Romans 6:1-4

In the New Testament, there is a spiritual principle that every Believer is in the process of dying to sin. This is God's expectation. You must realize that God knew that you could not live in your existing body with the sinful "self", because the sins that you commit will continue and continue and continue until you die. God had to do something to remove the control of sin. Please understand this. God made you into a new creation by sending His own Son to die on the cross. He knows you cannot control the "self" in you. It will take the power of the Holy Spirit. This is all a part of God's grace.

Most Christians think of the death of Jesus on the cross as a global event that permitted all sins to be forgiven. This is absolutely and totally true. But, God did not stop with the future salvation that Christians will experience when they do not have to face God's judgment at the end times. God used the cross, burial, and resurrection of Jesus to tell Christians that NOW is the time to apply God's work to our lives so that we will live a life like Christ. This is why you need to have GRACE always in the front of your mind.

In the passage above, it is explained that Christians died to sin and were baptized into Christ Jesus. Baptism is a transliterated word from the Greek. This means that it is the same word in Greek as it is in any other language. No new word was formed to replace the word baptism. At the time of Christ, "baptizo" was a word used to dye cloth. This usually meant placing the cloth completely under the dye solution. Therefore, to be baptized into Christ Jesus is to become like Him. In a way, you can say we are the same dyed (died) color as Christ. I believe it would be the color red representing the blood of Christ.

What makes this so important to you today is that God meant for this to happen to you when you became a Christian. God expects you to be baptized into Christ Jesus as soon as you become a Christian. This outward sign demonstrates that you and Christ Jesus are the same. You are identified with Him in every way. As an aside, this is why Jesus said that He had to be baptized...He wanted to identify with you as a human being. He wanted you to know that He was living a life just like you with all of the joys, trials, sufferings, temptations, and everything else that we experience in life. He experienced everything (and more) that you experience in life.

But, God does not stop here. God specifically says that you were baptized into the death of Jesus Christ. Do not make this hard to understand. God wanted you to begin to identify with Jesus in all that happened to Him starting with His death. You must think about this identification with Christ. You died as Christ died. God goes on to say that you were buried with Christ. This is another "renewing of the mind" concept that may be hard to accept, but God, through the Holy Spirit, will help you.

These identifications with Christ are the spiritual truths that God wants you to know about and apply to your life so that you will become more like Christ in the way you live. This is the goal that God has purposed for your life. He wants to remove the world from you and replace it with spiritual truths.

And we, who with unveiled faces all reflect the Lord's glory, are being transformed into his likeness with ever-increasing glory, which comes from the Lord, who is the Spirit. 2 Corinthians 3:8

God continues to draw a parallel between your new creation and Christ by saying that just as Christ was raised from the dead, you will live a new life. I believe that your new life is now. All Christians should be aware of these most important spiritual truths. They should be made a part of your everyday activity.

I think you will agree with the following statement: most people who become Christians and are baptized never make the connection that God is creating them new through their identification with Christ. I think it should be a huge part of every new Christian's life. They have died, been buried, and raised to a new life just like Christ. Most importantly, I think God expects this to be happening in the here and now.

There is one very damaging aspect of these spiritual truths. Too many Christians try to live a Christian life on their own strength. I hope this discussion has shown how that is impossible. Everything has been connected to the Son of God, because God said that this is the way it is going to work and it is the only way it's going to work.

Every Christian should be seeking what Christ did, how He lived with other people, how He responded to good and bad things, etc. Only then can we truly become the children of God on this earth giving a great and true witness of who God is and how much He loves you and others.

I hope this has given you something to think about in your own life. No matter how long you have been a Christian, please do not rationalize that it is too late to live a life for God as He intended. If you are a Christian and you make these spiritual truths part of your life, I hope you will seek out a new Christian who has been recently baptized. I beg you to walk along side them and explain this unbelievable grand plan that God put in place for us to live a Christ-like life today. This is the same life that He wants you to live now!

6. Faith is a make or break in your relationship with God

And without faith it is impossible to please God, because anyone who comes to him must believe that he exists and that he rewards those who earnestly seek him. Hebrews 11:6

Everything that concerns your relationship with God and other people draws its strength from the amount of faith that you have. There is an illustration that I have found very useful in explaining a person's position in this world and in the spiritual realm. Although an over simplification, below is an illustration of the two aspects of your life: the world and the Spirit.

Spirit

World

This illustration is very useful for plotting where you place your faith: in the world or in the Spirit. You can also use it to help you see God's perspective on critical parts of your life versus what the world says. For example, you can define "love" in the world (romantic) as compared to the Spirit (unconditional with no feelings involved.) Is your life centered on the spiritual or the worldly definition of "love"?

God expects Believers to continually grow in their faith. Without faith it is impossible to please God. Everything that you will learn that is significant to your life and your relationship to the Lord comes down to the strength of faith in your life. The first few years of your life consist of living in the world with very little living in the Spirit. As a result, the world becomes dominant in how you live your life. You will place your faith in those things in the world that appear to offer you security, comfort, and happiness.

When you become a Christian, God expects you to be transformed with the renewing of your mind (see Romans 12:1-2). He expects your faith to be transferred from the things of this world to His kingdom. Hopefully, you will be obedient to God as you learn about who He is and His priorities.

As you strive toward becoming more Christ-like in your behavior, the things below the line representing the world will no longer influence you. Instead, the things that are spiritual will become more important in how you live your life. As you exercise your faith in God, your outlook on life begins to orient itself toward God's perspective. You understand to the point that there is a spiritual change in your life. You will begin to put the focus of your faith on the spiritual. You must allow this to occur to grow spiritually. Without faith, it is impossible to please God.

7. God works everything for the good of those who love Him

"And we know that in all things God works for the good of those who love him, who have been called according to his purpose." Romans 8:28

Many believers are aware of this verse and have used it in times of trouble for encouragement. It contains a powerful truth about God. When there are problems in our lives, we become so inwardly focused on our selves that we forget about doing God's work, even though God continues to work within our lives to make us more Christ-like. God has never promised the "good" life that we envision should be ours just because we are God's. God's work is to reveal Himself to everyone on this earth through every good thing possible including you. I am astounded at the power and sovereignty of God to take anything negative and work it out to the good of our lives.

It's not that we stop loving Him; it's just that our worldly problems seem to overwhelm us. All too often, we want things to be good here on this earth ignoring that God is working in all things; even in the things that we would consider as negative. The antidote to this "self consuming" outlook on life is to comprehend the power of God in "all things," and to know that He will stop at nothing to bring you (and everyone else) closer to Him. When we realize this, we can begin to see and understand the purpose that God has for our lives: love God and serve others. These thoughts require a constant renewing of the mind.

While living in Florida, God moved our family to New York. It was difficult to see God's purpose for such a drastic move for people who grew up in Georgia. However, looking back on that move, there are so many God-things that happened that made our whole family more dependent on God, and one another. As an example, a men's mentor has maintained a spiritual relationship with me for the past 20 years: every Thursday night, we talk to one another and share our prayer needs. God knows what we need years before we need it, and He gives us the opportunities to see something good that would normally had been considered bad.

God says that when someone loves Him, He will make things happen that will result "for the good" within the life of that person in the Kingdom of God. The "love him" part is what Believers confess. But what about those "who have been called according to his purpose?"

As a Believer, you belong to God, and He has a purpose for your life that is part of His plan to produce good works in your life. God works in our lives as we deny ourselves (our own problems) and trust Him for everything. God's purpose in your life is for you to get yourself out of the way, and allow Him to work through you so that others will come to know Him. When that happens, all things will be good.

God is so powerful that He can take the pains, troubles, and bad circumstances that occur in your life in this world and make something good that will last for eternity. If you have given this verse to others as encouragement, then take it for yourself as an encouragement. Allow God to work through your "problems". My advice is to "get out of God's way, and let Him work through you," resulting in His good will.

8. Think about the hope in the Glory of God

Therefore, since we have been justified through faith, we have peace with God through our Lord Jesus Christ, through whom we have gained access by faith into this grace in which we now stand. And we boast in the hope of the glory of God. Romans 5:1-2

The verses above should make you so joyful that you would want to do cartwheels. I continue to be amazed by God for what He has done so that we can actually see Him one day. No one can see God and live unless they are without sin; i.e., been made righteous as He is righteous. These verses should fill you with joy, peace, and love.

God has justified us through our faith. The word "justified" means that God has provided a way for us to live with Him in heaven. We are justified through our faith in His Son, Jesus Christ. Our faith is our belief that Jesus is the Son of God. Our faith also includes the fact that the Son of God entered our world to live a life just like we live on this earth. He worked as a carpenter, so He suffered splinters in His hands from working with wood. He grew physically tired as he labored over a certain piece of furniture in shaping it to be useful. He had to bathe to wash away the sweat, dirt, and grime that were part of His work. The Bible says that He was tempted in all of the ways that we face temptation. However, He remained sinless. He never disobeyed God. He only did what God, the Father, told Him to do. He remained righteous His entire earthly life.

We, on the other hand, quickly give into temptations and become unrighteous or ungodly. There is no way we can wash away the stain of our sins. There is no way we can work hard enough to be forgiven of our sins. There is no way that we can always do what God tells us to do. We are rebels from God's point of view. Thankfully, Jesus Christ willingly became an innocent sacrifice on the cross for all of our sins. It is because of our faith in what Jesus did that we will be able to stand before God, and tell Him that we believe that Christ died for our sins. It is with that faith that we are justified to God. There is no other way!

Since we are now justified before God, we have peace with God. Do not underestimate this peace. God is a wrathful God concerning sin. Revelation 20 speaks of a day coming when everyone will stand before God and give an accounting of their works. We, as Christians, will have Christ as our mediator between God and us. Our faith in Christ will permit Christ to intercede for you in front of God and you will not suffer God's wrath for your sins. Those without faith in Christ will attempt to give their own life's account of why they have earned their way to be justified before God. God will not accept their works as a substitute for faith in Christ. After giving their account of their works, they will feel the wrath of God as they are thrown into the Lake of Fire and be eternally separated from the love of God.

We, on the other hand, will spend eternity with God because of the grace that we will experience from God. This grace will be so powerful that nothing on this earth can compare to what we will experience. It will be immeasurable joy, peace, and love that we will experience when we are in heaven. It is these kinds of thoughts that Christians need to have now on this earth to live a life like Christ. When we allow our minds to dwell on the things of this earth (good and bad), we miss the image of the grace that we now have because of Jesus Christ.

The verses above conclude with the results of thinking about being justified and standing in the grace from God. We will have positive thoughts about the glory of God. This glory is brighter, cleaner, purer, and stronger than any light and/or power that exists on this earth. The brightness given off by a nuclear explosion is darkness compared to the glory of God that we will experience. I don't know about you, but the more I think about this kind of glory, the more I want to go on to be with Him. I would go so far to say that is how God expects us to live on this earth. His expectation of a Christian is that we are so strongly convicted about being in the Presence of God; our life here on this earth is lived in the light of the hope of that glory.

I think this would cause many Christians to experience events that would renew their minds. I believe that their integrity, their values, their purpose in life, and the way they relate to others would be dramatically changed by the thoughts of this hope of glory. Their priorities would undergo dramatic changes. Their use of resources (time and money) would become totally "unworldly", meaning that their view of worldly resources would change from self-consumption to

God-oriented activities. Christians with the hope of glory in their minds would live a life like "aliens" to the people living in the world. Other people may view them as unrealistic or just plain "crazy" by the kinds of decisions that they make.

The Bible called for the Hebrews to be different and God calls the "church" (body of Believers) to be different. This difference is called being "holy". Examine your life as a Christian and evaluate how God would rate you as being "holy." Holiness in the world today is achievable by a Christian as long as they focus on the hope of the glory of God.

9. God expects you to become a holy witness for Him

Rejoice always, pray continually, give thanks in all circumstances; for this is God's will for you in Christ Jesus. Do not quench the Spirit. Do not treat prophecies with contempt but test them all; hold on to what is good, reject every kind of evil. 1 Thessalonians 5:16-25

These are some of the most uplifting verses you can find in the Bible. There are three commands given to every Believer: Rejoice, Pray, and Give Thanks. There is a time component assigned to each of these: Always, Continually, and In All Circumstances. These commands actually consist of three verses. It would be prudent if you could memorize these three very short verses. There is no way you can say these verses to yourself without experiencing a personal renewal of the mind. "Rejoice always" does not leave any room for pity parties or "woe is me." There is no room for rehashing all of your illnesses for the last six years or 20 years or ever how long. There's no need to rehash the jobs you have had and not had. God expects you to REJOICE always!

As you are rejoicing always, you should also be praying continually. This does not leave much time in the day, does it? If you are already thinking that this is impossible for you to do, God has you exactly where He wants you. With God, nothing is impossible. So, let's get on with it. Let's get that rejoicing going with praises to God and the music that lifts Him high as the God of the Universe. Let's remember those people in small Bible Study groups that are going through really difficult times. Pray for events throughout the world.

Also, we are to give thanks in all circumstances. Here we go again! God asks a lot of us Believers through His Word. I don't know about you, but when

I first read this, my mind jumped to bad circumstances. Then it jumped to good circumstances because it is easy to give thanks for the good times. But no...God had to include the word "all". I remember in the movie, "Facing the Giants", the coach told his team that they would praise God for the good times, and they would praise God for the bad times. I will guarantee you that your mind will be full of the glory of God and the radiance of Jesus Christ through the power of the Holy Spirit will consume all of your negative emotions and thoughts. I think that sounds a lot better than to be down and depressed with everyone I meet. Let me Rejoice, Pray and Give Thanks so that I am prepared to help someone else out of the despair and depression where Satan loves to see us waddle in. Renew your mind!

Now, God calls these three commands as being in the will of God. WOW!! Here I've been searching all over the Bible for God's will for my life, and He gives it to me in these three simple verses. However, He does not stop there. He adds some deep spiritual activities that every Believer needs to be involved with every day of their life. Unfortunately, I do not think many of us Believers are doing a good job with these spiritual ones. You can almost hear God telling Moses not to quench the Spirit by throwing water on the Burning Bush. This is like a fire that is trying to be put out, and you throw water or sand on the fire to put it out completely. Never be a Holy Spirit Quencher. Let Gatorade quench your thirst, but do not let anything quench the Holy Spirit working in you or someone else. In the case of God's work, we should always allow the Holy Spirit to continue to use His power when spiritual things are happening. It is not a good time to say that you need to get home because dinner is in the stove or kick-off is at 1:00. We do not need to look like we are in a hurry to leave when people are responding to the call of Almighty God. Do not be a Spirit Quencher.

At the same time, we need to know the prophecies and not treat them flippantly. Each chapter in the Book of 1 Thessalonians ends with a prophecy regarding the Second Coming of Christ. This is probably the most agreed upon prophecy by all of the churches and denominations in the world. Even the Jews are still waiting His first coming. Also, if you will read all of 1 Thessalonians 4, you will find a description of what some Believers call the Rapture. This is when Jesus will call the church to come to heaven. This does not mean that a lot of church buildings will disappear, but rather, a lot of people will be absent from work; all children will be missing; and, there will be a lot of empty seats on Mass transit. All Believers will leave this earth in the twinkling of an eye, and will find themselves in the Presence of Jesus Christ in Heaven. This is beginning to sound really exciting and makes you want to be a part of that rapture.

Do you think this is why God has given us these commands in these verses: rejoice always – Why? Jesus is coming; pray continually – Why?–Jesus is coming; give thanks in all circumstances – Why? Jesus is coming; do not quench the Holy Spirit – Why?–Jesus is coming! God has given us the greatest prophecy of all time: Jesus is coming again! God has given us tools to help us to be a holy witness for God. It always comes down to "do it!" It is an imperative for all Believers to experience a renewing of the mind about the Second Coming of Christ.

Finally, as Believers, we are to hold on to everything that is good. Now, I come from a small town in Georgia called "Douglasville". It has now been swallowed up by Atlanta as a part of the Metropolitan area. Since it was a small town, there were not very many lessons on what is good and what is bad. Most children usually passed things around and got a real good worldly education. What I am saying is that most people know the difference between good and bad. However, reread the verses again very carefully. Similar to the Sermon on the Mount when Jesus said, "you have heard it has been said"..."but I tell you". Jesus took murder and gave a deeper definition of murder as being anger in your mind. He took adultery and defined it as the evil thoughts in the mind about the opposite or same sex.

In other words, there is a higher calling to be a disciple of Christ. If you are a true Believer of Jesus Christ, you do not want to have the appearance of having done evil. It is to go so far as to make sure that no one can misunderstand or misinterpret anything you say or do as being evil. For example, a man at work who takes a woman (who is not his wife) out to lunch to deliver a performance appraisal can be easily misunderstood. A woman who seems to talk a lot about "free marriage" could easily be accused of listening to the world or reading worldly books.

As you can see by these verses, Christians are to be held to a higher standard but not for salvation. You are to be held to a higher standard (to be holy) so that other people will get to know who God is, what Christ did on the Cross, and how the Holy Spirit provides power to live a glorious and abundant life on this earth. You might want to do a "holiness" check with your own behavior. I pray you have a truthful and confidential mentor who could speak the truth to you about how others see Christ in you.

10. You MUST reach the spiritual fullness of Christ in the body of Christ

When you ascended on high, you took many captives; you received gifts from people, even from the rebellious—that you, Lord God, might dwell there. Psalm 68:18

But to each one of us grace has been given as Christ apportioned it. This is why it says: "When he ascended on high, he took many captives and gave gifts to his people."(What does "he ascended" mean except that he also descended to the lower, earthly regions? He who descended is the very one who ascended higher than all the heavens, in order to fill the whole universe.) So Christ himself created the Body of Christ (you and me) to equip his people for works of service, so that the body of Christ may be built up until we all reach unity in the faith and in the knowledge of the Son of God and become mature, attaining to the whole measure of the fullness of Christ.

Then we will no longer be infants, tossed back and forth by the waves, and blown here and there by every wind of teaching and by the cunning and craftiness of people in their deceitful scheming. Instead, speaking the truth in love, we will grow to become in every respect the mature body of him who is the head, that is, Christ. From him the whole body, joined and held together by every supporting ligament, grows and builds itself up in love, as each part does its work. Ephesians 4:7-16

Read these Bible passages again and again. Dwell and meditate on them. These are extremely important Bible passages in connecting the prophecy of Christ in the Old Testament with actual events in the New Testament. I hope you can understand how they directly impact the Body of Christ. Before Christ died on the cross for the sins of everyone, all saints could not enter into the Presence of God. The blood of Christ had not covered their sins. The people were unholy in the sight of a Holy God. When Christ died for the payment of mankind's sins, He descended to the lower, earthly regions to bring those who were now declared righteous to fill the whole universe. This is a "spiritual mystical event" in the life of a Believer (Abraham, Sarah, Isaac, Joseph, and many more), because they were now allowed to stand in the presence of the God, the One without sin. They were considered "holy" and without sin. I hope you will become comfortable in describing "spiritual and mystical events" in your life. It is an imperative that these words become part of your vocabulary as well as your thinking. By not using these words in normal conversation, you weaken your faith and belief in God. This definition requires a renewing of the mind.

The connection between the passage in Psalms and the passage in Ephesians is that Christ was preparing His Bride (the Body of Christ) for the End Times. He described the various roles that each of us will serve one another for Christ. We will no longer be infants tossed back and forth by every form of teaching. We will grow to become in every respect the mature body of the one who is the head, Christ. This body will continue to grow in Christ in maturity and build itself up in love as each one of us does our work.

This is not talking about the earthly body, but is describing the "spiritual mystical body" that every Believer will experience. Christ will be intimately involved in the changing of the earthly body into a spiritual body that will become mature reaching the fullness of Christ. This gives me a hope beyond anything this world could give. It sets my mind on spiritual things and not the things of this earth. "Come, Lord Jesus."

11. Be intentional about growing spiritually

To live in a manner worthy of the Lord, so as to be fully pleasing, in every good work bearing fruit and growing in the knowledge of God, strengthened with every power, in accord with his glorious might, for all endurance and patience, with joy giving thanks to the Father, who has made you fit to share in the inheritance of the holy ones in light. (NABRE) Colossians 1:10-12

And we pray this in order that you may live a life worthy of the Lord and may please Him in every way, bearing fruit in every good work, growing in the knowledge of God, being strengthened with all power according to his glorious might so that you may have great endurance and patience, and joyfully giving thanks to the Father, who has qualified you to share in the inheritance of the saints in the kingdom of light. (NIV) Colossians 1:10-12

Almost everyone tries to figure out what they want to do with their life. Early on, people ask, "What do you want to be when you grow up?" The same question can be asked about your spiritual life. If you wanted a career in a certain field, you would focus on education and jobs in that field. You intentionally prepare yourself to do something and to do it to the best of your ability.

"What are you becoming" in your spiritual life? Is there anything "intentional" about what you do to prepare yourself to live the most important life on this side of eternity? I challenge you to think about the specific activities that you do that you would classify as "spiritual growth." Are they intentional to help you grow deeper and stronger in your relationship with God? Or, are there things that you repeat and repeat and repeat with no significant spiritual change occurring in your life.

In the verses above, there are several things listed that would be considered as "spiritual growth." You are to live a life worthy of the Lord, and please Him in every way. Have you ever considered your life in this way? Reflect over the past week, and ask yourself if God would be pleased with what He saw in your life. There can be a big difference between doing something for the church and doing something for God. Good works (those done for God) will produce spiritual fruit. Fruit always includes a spiritual change in another person or in you. It may be as tremendous as someone accepting Christ, or it could mean giving hope to someone who is in despair.

God also wants you to get to know Him. This can only be done as you allow the Holy Spirit to show you spiritual things. Studying the life of Christ in the Bible is a great way to get to know God, because Jesus said that if you know Him, then you would know the Father. God has given you the Holy Spirit to help you grow spiritually. How often do you rely on the Spirit? How often do you ask God through the Holy Spirit to give you strength or spiritual knowledge?

The most important aspect of any Believer's life is to be constantly growing spiritually. Any time a Believer becomes entangled in this world or in themselves, it is impossible for that Believer to please God. Read Romans 12:1-2. Commit these verses to memory, and live them everyday of your life. You will experience life-changing events for the remainder of your earthly life. Be intentional about your spiritual life, because God expects it!

Section 2

A Biblical Perspective Of Who You Are

Introduction

A major part of a Believer's life is spent reflecting on being Christ-like in all of their affairs. The way we conduct our lives, as reflections of the spiritual realm may be the only testimony many people will receive about God. Only by daily study of God's Word can one know what are the actions of Christ that should be a part of their lives. For example, Jesus told a group that if someone asked them to walk a mile, they should walk two miles. At the time of Christ, a Roman soldier could force a Jew to carry something for a mile. Obviously, this was not well received by the Jews. Jesus went further with obedience to the Roman solider by saying that you should walk two miles. One mile was expected while two miles would have made an impression on the Roman solider.

This is the theme of all of the instructions of Christ. They consisted of denying self and making a sacrifice for others. This is the exact opposite of the philosophy of the world. "SELF" is the major component of people's lives. We are overwhelmed with ads, news media, movies, magazines, etc. about how you should look, how you should think, what you should own, and where you should go to please the "SELF" in you. It is extremely hard to even identify that self is sitting on the throne in your life telling you how you should live.

1. God expects you to become more Christ-like

Finally, brothers, we earnestly ask and exhort you in the Lord Jesus that, as you received from us how you should conduct yourselves to please God—and as you are conducting yourselves—you do so even more. For you know what instructions we gave you through the Lord Jesus. 1 Thessalonians 4:1-2

Christ wants to be on the throne of your life. As you conduct yourself in your life, you receive the instructions and commands of Christ through the Holy Spirit. Only in this way can you begin to eliminate the stronghold of self in your life. I am afraid that most Christians live from day to day with no thought of the commands of Christ. Do some personal Bible study by discovering what those commands are in the Bible. Make them a part of your heart and mind. Your behavior will change from "SELF" to Christ as you experience the freedom that the commands of Christ provide, as opposed to the world. Do not become a slave to your "SELF". A Christian controlled by the self is the most disgusting, most selfish, most arrogant, the angriest, and most jealous person as seen by others. God wants to remove these things from your life.

It should become apparent to you if you are living your life for your "SELF" or for Christ. When you realize that it is the self in you that controls you, you will realize that you are a slave to bad habits and selfish attitudes. Only after putting the commands of Christ in your life will you experience freedom, joy, and peace. You will also be the witness that God has called all Believers to be.

2. God created man in three parts: body, soul, and spirit

May God himself, the God of peace, sanctify you through and through. May your whole spirit, soul and body be kept blameless at the coming of our Lord Jesus Christ. 1 Thessalonians 5:23

This is a wonderful prayer that Paul gave to the people in a city called Thessalonica. Paul is asking for God to "sanctify" the people. Sanctify means to work with the people to become different from the world. To be made holy is another way of saying "to sanctify." God intends for every Believer to go through a metamorphosis to become more Christ-like in their behavior. This will require a change in the soul that will be manifested in the body. Someone with an unpleasing personality will not be easy to be around. Someone who has a negative attitude will exhibit similar negative traits in their facial and body movements, and, especially, with what they say about others. God expects a Believer to love God and to serve others as Christ lived on this earth.

The verse continues with a definition of a human being as three parts: spirit, soul, and body. A human being is a complex creation of God. After God created Adam, the Bible says: "Then the Lord God formed a man from the dust of the ground and breathed into his nostrils the breath of life, and the man became a living being." Genesis 2:7

"The breath of life" is unique to the creation of man. God did not do this for any of His other creations. Consider the "breath of life" as your soul. He had created the body out of dust, but instead of being a lump of clay, He went further. In Genesis 1:26, the Bible records, "Then God said, "Let us make mankind in our image, in our likeness."

In our likeness refers to the Trinity. I know it does not say "Trinity", but we know that God the Father, the Son, and the Holy Spirit is an eternal Trinity. God made man and woman in that likeness. This likeness is also unique to mankind. There is no other creation like mankind. The angels, all of the animals, and everything that God created is not like a human being. Mankind's likeness is the ability to think and reason. It is the need for relationships with others. Just as the Father, Son, and Holy Spirit are One, God intends all Believers to be as one (see John 17).

His likeness also includes a tremendous characteristic called the "free will". As we know man's free will is a wonderful aspect of man. We can choose to spend quality time with others. We can choose to help someone even if it requires a sacrifice on our part. But, man's free will has the potential for disaster, because man can reject God. Each aspect of man (body, soul, and spirit) will be discussed in this Section. I pray that these discussions will change your perspective on several things about who you are.

3. What is your soul?

May God himself, the God of peace, sanctify you through and through. May your whole spirit, soul and body be kept blameless at the coming of our Lord Jesus Christ. 1 Thessalonians 5:23

The soul is not a physical attribute of the body. It is what defines your personality. The soul consumes huge volumes of information as we grow from a baby to adulthood. Our soul collects facts that eventually determine our behavior. Our behavior has a tremendous impact on our relationships with others and God. The soul consists of the way we think and reason, the way we react emotionally to situations, and how we choose to live our life.

The soul is frequently considered as your personality. The soul carries the image of our consciousness, memories, and dreams. Our desires and wants are collected in our souls. From this information, we develop our life purpose, our goals, and a picture of how we see ourselves. You can summarize all of the aspects of your soul by saying that the soul is what makes you different and unique from other human beings.

At birth, our soul begins to form its identity. As we age through childhood and adolescence, our soul or personality becomes more defined. It does this because we all make decisions about the world around us. When a child is deprived of a basic human need, that child will develop a defense mechanism to protect themselves mentally and emotionally. Those defense mechanisms begin to shape our personalities that carry over into adulthood. You can refer to someone as a "quiet, introverted" person that is a result of some events that occurred in childhood or adolescence.

You choose your friends based on their personality. Of course, physical appearance plays an early role in friendship. However, a deeper relationship will be determined by the personalities (souls) of the people involved. If a person has a short temper, many of us would find it difficult to get close to such a person.

Interestingly, because we are human beings with a natural selfishness built into our souls, we usually look for how another person makes us feel as opposed to focusing on the needs of others. This is the motivating force behind the need to make friends. We need someone else to continually validate who we are as a human being. Our soul is at the center of this need.

Biblically speaking, God knows that we are basically selfish (sinners). He puts a huge amount of effort in trying to get us to see who we really are and who we should be as Christians. However, to change one's personality is very difficult in today's modern world where self is highly regarded and considered as having no problems. In summary, your soul is made up of your mind, emotions, and will. Your mind lets others know how you think and reason. Your emotions show how you react to given situations. Your will reveals the internal decisions that you make and say "this is who I really am...like it or leave me alone!"

4. The soul of a human being

Though you have not seen him, you love him; and even though you do not see him now, you believe in him and are filled with an inexpressible and glorious joy, for you are receiving the end result of your faith, the salvation of your souls. 1 Peter 1:8-9

There are basically two meanings for the word "soul" in the Bible. An example of one meaning is contained in the verses above that treat your soul as an entity within you that will experience salvation. It is what we mean when we refer to life in the physical body. In many translations, the Biblical word is translated as life instead of soul. "**What good is it for someone to gain the whole world, yet forfeit their life (soul)? Or what can anyone give in exchange for their life (soul)?"** (Mark 8:36-37) Another example is the following: **"And it came to pass, as her soul (life) was in departing, (for she died) that she called his name Benoni: but his father called him Benjamin.** (Genesis 35:18) We frequently say the phrase, "save a soul" in reference to evangelism. Again, what we are meaning is the life of an individual.

The second meaning is one that all Believers need to know. God created an amazing phenomenon that is the most unique aspect of all human beings. He created us in His image and **breathed** life into us and gave us a soul. The Biblical word used for soul means "breath". **"Then the Lord God formed a man from the dust of the ground and breathed into his nostrils the breath of life, and the man became a living being."** (Genesis 2:7) God desires a healthy relationship with us. However, everyone's soul is in trouble, and his or her personal relationship with God is in jeopardy.

When the woman saw that the fruit of the tree was good for food and pleasing to the eye, and also desirable for gaining wisdom, she took some and ate it. She also gave some to her husband, who was with her, and he ate it. Then the eyes of both of them were opened, and they realized they were naked; so they sewed fig leaves together and made coverings for themselves. (Genesis 3:6-7) **For all have sinned and fall short of the glory of God.** (Romans 3:23)

None of us can have a relationship with God because of the sin in our souls. However, God sent His Son, Jesus Christ, as a sacrifice for forgiveness of our sins. We must believe that He did that for us to have a relationship with Him. The difference between a Believer and an unbeliever is where their soul spends eternity. A Believer's soul will be spent with God while an unbeliever's soul will be separated from God for an eternity.

Most importantly, after we become a Believer, God expects to see our souls change to become more like Christ. This is a process that all Believers go through. All Believers should be diligent and aggressive in asking God to show them the changes needed to be made to their souls, and accept the leading of the Holy Spirit for those changes to take effect. However, most Believers are not working on becoming more Christ-like. This is a major weakness of Believers and is made prevalent by their non-Christ-like behavior that unbelievers see. The importance of soul changes for Believers to become more Christ-like is a major point of the New Testament.

5. The soul of Jesus Christ

Then he said to them, "My soul is overwhelmed with sorrow to the point of death. Stay here and keep watch with me." Matthew 26:38

"Now my soul is troubled, and what shall I say? 'Father, save me from this hour'? No, it was for this very reason I came to this hour. John 12:27

This section will give you an opportunity to compare your soul with the soul of Christ. Prepare to be honest about who you are as a personality. You do not hear many people talk about the soul of Jesus Christ, but we should. In the verses above, Jesus talked about His soul as being overwhelmed and being troubled. Have you ever thought of Jesus as having a soul (personality)? Do you have similar personality traits as Jesus? Examples of the personality of Jesus are the following:

The most important characteristic of the personality of Jesus was that He only did what God told Him to do. **Jesus gave them this answer: "Very truly I tell you, the Son can do nothing by himself; he can do only what he sees his Father doing, because whatever the Father does the Son also does.** (John 5:19) This is why He could claim that He was without sin. He was obedient to every word from God. Do you consciously strive to be obedient to God's Word?

Jesus did not seek any recognition for anything He did. He was full of humility. **"Be careful not to practice your righteousness in front of others to be seen by them. If you do, you will have no reward from your Father in heaven.** (Matthew 6:1) Do you have to share what you do for God or the church with others?

Jesus had no fear, because He had complete faith in God. **He said to his disciples, "Why are you so afraid? Do you still have no faith?"** (Mark 4:40) He expects His disciples to have complete faith also.

Jesus knew and had compassion for the needs of others and took action to satisfy those needs. **"I have compassion for these people; they have already been with me three days and have nothing to eat."** (Mark 8:2) The soul of Jesus aches about the needs of others. How is your soul impacted by the needs of others?

Jesus loved children and took time to care for them. **When Jesus saw this, he was indignant. He said to them, "Let the little children come to me, and do not hinder them, for the kingdom of God belongs to such as these.** (Mark 10:14-16) He does not like for adults to abuse children. Do you unintentionally frustrate or make fun of a child?

Jesus was adamant about people loving and serving God and others. **Jesus replied, "No one who puts a hand to the plow and looks back is fit for service in the kingdom of God."** (Luke 9:62) He expects His disciples to stay focused on God's purpose for them in living their life on this earth.

There are many, many more examples that describe the soul (personality) of our Lord, Jesus Christ. He expects for His disciples to learn of His personality and to make it part of their personality. This is what it means to become more

Christ-like. This is the spiritual work that all Believers should be doing through the power of the Holy Spirit. May I suggest that you spend some time reading and studying Matthew, Mark, Luke, and John to learn about the personality of Jesus Christ. Create your own list of the personality traits that you learn about Jesus Christ and about yourself. Section 3 contains several examples of applying God's Word to your life and experience a renewal of the mind.

6. Your soul is intended to become like Christ

And we all, who with unveiled faces contemplate the Lord's glory, are being transformed into his image with ever-increasing glory, which comes from the Lord, who is the Spirit. 2 Corinthians 3:18

Knowing that you are a sinner and that Christ died for the forgiveness of your sins is the major theme of the Bible. The verse above is clear that God is working on your soul to make it more like Christ. This is a major theme of the New Testament. As a Believer matures, he or she should be reflecting similar traits as the soul of Jesus Christ. The verse above also makes the ABSOLUTE TRUTH that these changes in your soul are accomplished only through the Holy Spirit.

"I have been crucified with Christ and I no longer live, but Christ lives in me. The life I now live in the body, I live by faith in the Son of God, who loved me and gave himself for me. I do not set aside the grace of God, for if righteousness could be gained through the law, Christ died for nothing!" Galatians 2:20-21

Too many Christians try to live like a Christian only to become very frustrated and, eventually, defeated over their repetitive attempts at changing themselves. So many Christians see the need to be more Christ-like, and they understand where they are weak in making those changes. This is not what God intended. He will make the changes in you. All you have to do is to decide to follow the leading of the Holy Spirit. This begins with the verse above where we are asked to consider ourselves crucified and dead.

What do we need to consider about ourselves as crucified and dead? Our souls (personalities) contain all of the elements to help us follow the law. The "law" consists of all of the rules that you have created in your soul to make you feel righteous. None of these rules are part of God's plan for you to live a life of freedom. The verses above are clear that it is not through the law that we obtain righteousness. It is only through the realization that you are dead and Christ is alive in you. When you became a Christian, the Holy Spirit filled the spiritual part of your life. You can make decisions (showing your personality) based on input from your mind and emotions or from the Holy Spirit who now dwells within you. When you choose to obey the Holy Spirit, your actions will be Christ-like. Others will see Christ in you! Your life will be producing the fruit of the Spirit. (Galatians 5:22-23)

Follow God's example, therefore, as dearly loved children and walk in the way of love, just as Christ loved us and gave himself up for us as a fragrant offering and sacrifice to God. (Ephesians 5:1-2) This summarizes what it means to have your personality in the same image as Jesus Christ – "walk in the way of love, just as Christ loved" you. This word love is the Greek word "agape" that means to serve others first especially when it requires a sacrifice on your part. Jesus sacrificed Himself for you, and God is now asking for you to sacrifice yourself for others. You will become a fragrant offering to God and to others. God will be pleased with your sacrifice.

7. The soul is the center of the spiritual war with the flesh

I do not understand what I do. For what I want to do I do not do, but what I hate I do. And if I do what I do not want to do, I agree that the law is good. As it is, it is no longer I myself who do it, but it is sin living in me. For I know that good itself does not dwell in me, that is, in my sinful nature. For I have the desire to do what is good, but I cannot carry it out. For I do not do the good I want to do, but the evil I do not want to do—this I keep on doing. Now if I do what I do not want to do, it is no longer I who do it, but it is sin living in me that does it. So I find this law at work: Although I want to do good, evil is right there with me. For in my inner being I delight in God's law; but I see another law at work in me, waging war against the law of my mind and making me a prisoner of the law of sin at work within me. Romans 7:15-23

The above passage explains why Christians continue to sin. You must read through this passage several times and read it very slowly. The passage is saying that your soul (mind and emotions) will enslave you to things that you think you must do as a Christian. However, you fail and do what you do not want to do, and you do not do what you should do. As a Believer, you are not alone. This is a statement of the spiritual warfare of all Believers. The flesh pulls at your will through your soul (mind and emotions). Although the Holy Spirit can provide the spiritual answer, a Believer allows the flesh to be stronger and follows its directions that are always sinful. You must put to death the flesh in your soul and rely only on the Holy Spirit to become more Christ-like.

The mind governed by the flesh is death, but the mind governed by the Spirit is life and peace. The mind governed by the flesh is hostile to God; it does not submit to God's law, nor can it do so. Those who are in the realm of the flesh cannot please God. (Romans 8:6-8)

This is another way of looking at the spiritual war that is ongoing in every Believer. ALL believers are fighting this spiritual war. The mind that is death means that only rotten stinking fruit is produced in your actions that others see. If you allow your mind to control you, then you are in a state of hostility with God. These are strong words, but the Bible makes it clear that you are either with God or against God. Every time you make a decision based on what you think or how you feel, you are giving power to the flesh and will be controlled by the flesh ending in sin. Consider the following verse:

If you do what is right, will you not be accepted? But if you do not do what is right, sin is crouching at your door; it desires to have you, but you must rule over it." (Genesis 4:7) This is what God told Cain before Cain killed his brother Abel. The word "desires" is a Hebrew word that means to take control. Cain had a choice to obey his emotions or to obey God. He chose his emotions. The moment he did that, sin took control of Cain, and he committed murder. This is the same situation that occurs numerous times every day for Believers. We are tempted by the flesh and choose to obey what our mind or emotions are saying instead of what the Holy Spirit is leading us to do.

What a wretched man I am! Who will rescue me from this body that is subject to death? Thanks be to God, who delivers me through Jesus Christ our Lord! (Romans 7:24-25) This is God's answer to our war with the flesh. He has given us Christ who was tempted in every way that we are tempted. However, He remained sinless, because the Holy Spirit led Him in all of His actions. God asks us to live a life in the image of Christ.

8. A Believer must care of his/her soul

What good is it for someone to gain the whole world, yet forfeit their soul? Or what can anyone give in exchange for their soul? Mark 8:36-37

Soul comes from the Greek word "psuche". You can see its closeness to our word "psyche". It means the "breath of life." A worldly definition that I favor is the following: psyche–the human soul, mind, or spirit. The soul could also be called your personality. A personality is a description of a person in how they think, feel, make decisions, their values, and so on. In other words, the soul of a person consists of their rational thinking, their emotional reactions, and their use of their will to make decisions.

Regrettably, our soul becomes very rigid as we age. If it is too rigid, we will become obstinate toward God and will not allow His Holy Spirit to guide us on needed changes in our life to become more Christ-like. This will cause problems in our relationship with God and with others.

When we first meet someone, we begin to judge whether we can like this person or not based only on their physical appearance. As we get to know a person, our soul will give us information to help us in our decision to like or not like that person. Our soul will evaluate how they express themselves. We can see how they react to difficult situations. We can hear the words they use, and judge whether they are edifying or tearing down others. Our souls will give information to our will to make decisions on how close do I want to be to that person. All of this causes disruptions in our relationship with others. It short-circuits any of God's plans for us to minister to that person. We would be living in the flesh and not in the Spirit.

Remember that your soul is collecting information your entire life. If you indulge your flesh by seeing certain unwholesome movies, TV shows, magazines, or books, you will have put those images into your soul. People who watch News programs on a daily basis can easily become depressed to the point of being a cynical view of life. This is not the attitude for a Believer to exhibit to anyone else. You must be on guard as to what can take control of your soul.

Jesus replied: "Love the Lord your God with all your heart and with all your soul and with all your mind." Matthew 22:37

I hope you begin to see clearly the soul that is within you is extremely important to who you are as a Believer. Jesus uses our soul to describe how much we are to love God. We are to love Him with all of our soul. With this kind of love in your soul, you will not be giving the flesh in you the opportunity to control who you are. I pray that you have been spiritually enlightened with the importance of your soul. I hope you see the need in your life to become more Christ-like in all that you do. This is sometimes referred to as, "Walk your talk!" In other words, be genuine and transparent with your personality so that others will see Jesus in you. In this way, your witness to others will be how you live through your personality or soul.

9. The difference between the soul and the spirit

For the word of God is alive and active. Sharper than any double-edged sword, it penetrates even to dividing soul and spirit, joints and marrow; it judges the thoughts and attitudes of the heart. Hebrews 4:12

This verse provides a description of man as being body (joints and marrow), soul, and spirit. 1 Thessalonians 5:23 also identify man as three parts: body, soul, and spirit. It is imperative for a Believer to understand the difference between their soul and their spirit. The soul is not the spirit and the spirit is not the soul. The soul consists of the mental intellect and the emotions that a person uses to decide their actions. The soul is what makes humans different from all other created beings. The soul is what makes humans different from the angels who are spirits only – they have no souls. The soul is what gives a person a unique personality. The soul is who a person is and gives them their individuality. If you think about the soul in this way, one can easily see that this is where the "flesh" resides in a person's life.

Those who live according to the flesh have their minds set on what the flesh desires; but those who live in accordance with the Spirit have their minds set on what the Spirit desires. The mind governed by the flesh is death, but the mind governed by the Spirit is life and peace. The mind governed by the flesh is hostile to God; it does not submit to God's law, nor can it do so. Those who are in the realm of the flesh cannot please God. Romans 8:5-8

The Bible speaks of "flesh" in two ways: 1) the body, and 2) the fallen part of our human nature residing in our soul. Our free will is influenced by the flesh in our soul or by our spirit. For example, in our soul, we intellectually decide that there is or is not a God, or we react to temptations that are appealing to the emotions in our soul. Sin takes control of who we are when the person's will, also part of the soul, decides to give in to the soul, and not the spirit.

You, however, are not in the realm of the flesh but are in the realm of the Spirit, if indeed the Spirit of God lives in you. And if anyone does not have the Spirit of Christ, they do not belong to Christ. Romans 8:9

Too many Believers base their relationship with God on the condition of their soul (mentally and emotionally) and not their spirit. God is a spirit and He deals with human beings spiritually in their spirit. Therefore, a person who becomes a Believer must realize that they are a sinner because of the flesh in their soul. God gives the Holy Spirit to indwell the Believer to provide another source to influence the free will of the Believer. For a Believer to hear the Spirit's leading, the soul must be humbled or, quite frankly, told to "Shut-up." Believers must not rely on their minds or emotions to grow spiritually.

For a Believer to grow spiritually, the soul is not the place to try to make changes. To become more Christ-like, a Believer must rely on the Spirit. Only input from the Spirit can have a spiritual influence on a Believer. A person can learn every verse in the Bible with no spiritual growth. A person can raise their hands in worship and shout "Hallelujah!" with no spiritual growth. Following your mind or your emotions is giving sin control of your behavior. Following the Holy Spirit will give you life and peace.

Section 3

Application Of Spiritual Truths To Become Christ-Like

Introduction

I believe all Believers experience rough times in living their life as a Christian. When these rough times occur, Believers begin to look for a quick fix, because that is the philosophy of this world. We look for a drug to ease the pain. We try to find some comforting words in a devotional or even the Bible. We expect others around us to understand that we are not operating on all cylinders of our beliefs. We begin to believe that we are alone on these feelings. When that happens, we can truly believe that God has deserted us or wants us to go through some kind of growing pain without Him.

Let me make this as clear as possible. Christians are not to look to the world for spiritual healing and growth. When your thoughts turn internal you will be messing up God's answer to your problems. Instead of living life using worldly activities, God wants to remind us that the heart of living a Christian life is all about love. "**Love** the Lord your **God** with all your heart and with all your soul and with all your mind and with all your strength." (Mark 12:30) "And now these three remain: faith, hope and **love**. But the greatest of these is **love**." (1 Corinthians 13:13)

The basis of any and all activity as a Believer must always start with love, and continue to increase in love constantly and continually. The reason God puts love as first in your life is that Christ died on the cross for your sins – love!

If you will always think of love first, your spiritual insight will grow in depth and in knowledge. You will have a spiritual insight that sees things as God sees them.

I repeat: most Believers choose the worldly philosophy to try to get back to feeling good or feeling that they are back in control. This is WRONG! It is LOVE! You do not pray; you do not read the Bible; you do not meet with your Pastor or others; you do not do anything unless you put love first. This will help you to discern what is the best way for you to live your Christian life. You will grow to be blameless, because your focus will be on God's love and the love of Christ. Unconditional love must come first in your life at all times and in all circumstances.

I cannot emphasize enough that what non-believers see in the lives of Believers is the same as the world's. They do not see unconditional love. They do not see a Believer offering glory and praise to God through their reaction to worldly problems. In His Word, God is clearly telling us to think of His love first in ALL THAT WE DO! A change in attitude is needed by Believers today for the gospel of Christ to be spread throughout the world. **"To the glory and praise of God."**

This section contains 31 Biblical examples that compare and contrast a worldly mind with a Christ-like mind. Each example provides Bible passages that can be used as references to the specific behavior or attitude that is being described. This is not a section that I suggest you read in one sitting. As you read through them, attempt to identify those behaviors and attitudes that the Holy Spirit is emphasizing to you as part of your life. You may want to try to prioritize them so that you can focus on the ones that need attention. You will find that the applications of the Bible verses are easy to apply to your life. In many examples, I describe personal examples to help you make changes in your life. This section would also encourage good discussions in a small Bible Study group.

One way to read through these is as a monthly devotional. I have outlined all the topics contained in this chapter below:

Introduction

1. Believers consider all things as lost

2. Keep your hands clean and your heart pure

3. Revenge is God's and His alone
4. Anger should not be a part of a Believer's life
5. Believers can do all things
6. Humility means living your life under God's Authority
7. Believers are not grumblers
8. What is the basis of your faith?
9. Do you respect God?
10. God's promises in your life
11. When Christians stop witnessing, God judges
12. Love one another
13. Obedience and Disobedience
14. Do not grow weary; God's love endures forever
15. Pride is the sin of all sins
16. God will rescue you
17. Maintain your relationship to always be near God
18. All of our sins are removed by the blood of Christ
19. Spiritual battles are being waged all around you
20. Thankfulness should be a permanent attitude for all Believers
21. Meditate on God's Word to learn of Him
22. Where your focus should be

23. Do not trust in people – only in God
24. Know the TRUTH
25. Unforgiving is NOT a Christ-like attitude
26. What are you doing with your wealth?
27. No place for worry in a Believer's Life
28. Fellowship with other Believers
29. Quietness in your soul
30. Practical living in today's world
31. God intentionally tests your faith through suffering

1. Believers consider all things as lost

But whatever were gains to me I now consider loss for the sake of Christ. What is more, I consider everything a loss compared to the surpassing greatness of knowing Christ Jesus my Lord, for whose sake I have lost all things. I consider them rubbish, that I may gain Christ. Philippians 3:7-8

Paul wrote these words as a summary of his life after he had accepted Jesus Christ as his Lord and Savior. These verses are extremely difficult to live out in our lives today as Believers in America. We desire everything in our lives today to be a gain. We always want to be on the positive side of obtaining wealth. It is the culture that we live in.

When a person accepts Christ, there begins a journey for that person to begin thinking spiritually instead of worldly. The verses above are clear that whatever a Believer thinks was valuable before they became a Christian is now considered as a loss in their life. This is definitely out of this world thinking. Many of us become prideful over our children, or our homes, or our cars, or our job title. All of these things have been replaced with the simple fact of knowing Christ Jesus as Lord. This should be a common purpose for all Believers as we allow the

Holy Spirit to work in us to transform the way we think. Many Christians do not consider all that will happen to them when they accept Christ. The transforming of the mind is huge to become a living witness for God.

Consider those people who track the stock market on a daily basis. They are driven to always be gaining. When the market declines, they begin to panic and do everything they can to reduce the loss. What do you think Paul's perspective of the stock market would be? Suppose Paul invested in the market and experienced a loss. I tend to think that it would not bother him in the least bit, because his life's focus was on Christ. He would call his loss "rubbish." I know some of you are saying, "But that's my life savings!" Read those words again and ask how your life is saved. It is saved by the sacrifice of Christ on the cross, not by how much money you have in a portfolio of stocks. Your mind should begin a transformation from worldly thinking to spiritual thinking.

Another aspect of our lives today is the market value of our homes. Only in America could the perceived value of your home dictate your value in society. The bigger, the fancier, and the more landscaped your home is, the "wealthier" you will appear to others. If Paul owned one of those houses, how would he view it? He would probably downsize to fit his lifestyle. (In his case, it would likely be a tent.)

Read the verses above again and you will find that the transforming of your mind will result in your considering your house as no longer a possession of yours. There is nothing wrong about anyone's house and the cost of that house. There is something wrong if we have set our hearts on appearing "well-off" because of our homes. Our hearts should be focused on Christ and those things in heaven, not the things of this earth. Allow your mind to begin to seek the eternal possessions that God has given you.

2. Keep your hands clean and your heart pure

And the Word of God says,

Who may ascend the mountain of the Lord? Who may stand in his holy place? The one who has clean hands and a pure heart, who does not trust in an idol or swear by a false god. Psalm 24:3-4

I equate the first two questions of the above Bible passage to a Believer's growth in Christ. God does not wish for anyone to perish; i.e., experience eternal death or eternal separation from God. At the same time, He is strongly adamant that those who become Believers should make it their life purpose to change their behavior to be more Christ-like. As a Believer, I like the idea of ascending to God and standing in His holy place. Eastern religions have a similar idea with the exception that you may only find a wise man at the top of the mountain. In the case of a Believer, you will find God as you actively seek Him.

The next sentence of the above Bible passage tells you how to seek God and find Him. It says that the seeker must have clean hands. Of course, all of us wash our hands several times per day (especially during flu season.) But this reference to "clean hands" must be a reference to something spiritual. What do you allow your hands to do that will result in sin? You may use a remote to get to certain ungodly TV programs. There are too many younger Christians who feel they must watch the same sitcoms as their Christ-less friends. These sitcoms espouse only garbage that clutters the mind and neglects your life purpose. Your hands can pick up the wrong kind of book or magazine. God desires you to worship Him with raised hands signifying a need for Him. Do not let it be dirty hands.

What follows the misuse of your hands is an impure heart. Whatever you have been reading or watching can easily become a set of chemical reactions in your brain that will be repeated as bad memories. This chemical program of some ungodly event can haunt your memory for years. It is impossible to keep your heart pure. Reading the Bible, being in a Christian environment with other Believers, and experiencing a quiet time with God will help you guard your mind and heart.

Finally, the easiest way to fail to seek God is to have other things in your life that you consider more important. We usually don't call them idols, but that is what they are. God is a jealous God and desires for you to put Him first in your life at all times and all the time. Seek God with clean hands and a pure heart, and you will be living an abundant life amidst a sinful world.

3. Revenge is God's and His alone

Do not take revenge, my dear friends, but leave room for God's wrath, for it is written: "It is mine to avenge; I will repay," says the Lord. Romans 12:19

"'Do not seek revenge or bear a grudge against anyone among your people, but love your neighbor as yourself. I am the Lord. Leviticus 19:18

I can get so mad at other people for what they do. When someone abuses a child, I go ballistic and want to teach that person a lesson in the same way they are mistreating a child. Speeding hogs that drive like they were on your bumper can cause road rage in you. (BTW: never reach the "road rage" level, and never ever get out of your car to confront someone else. You don't know what they have in their glove compartment.) There are numerous times in most of humanity where revenge is all we can think about toward another person. We want to take the law into our own hands. We plot how we can be avenged. We want to be the police, the judge, the jury, and the executioner. BUT, this is not what God wants for you.

In all situations, God would desire for you to be at peace. He relieves us of the motive for revenge, because He makes it plain that He will take revenge against those who abuse others. Child abuse, in any form, is one of my hot buttons. God says He will take the perpetrator, tie a millstone around their neck, and throw them into the ocean. "Yah! God!"

God knows the weakness of our flesh. When we allow the flesh to take control of our mouth, our arms and our hands, we could get into some serious trouble. First of all, we are not being Christ-like. We should remember Christ being brutally beaten by the Roman soldiers. He should have died from the beatings, but that was not God's plan. Christ had to die on the cross for our sins to be forgiven. Peter tried to stop the Jewish police from arresting Jesus, and Peter lashed out with his sword and cut off one the men's ears. Jesus healed that ear.

I hope you are beginning to realize that God wants you to remove the flesh that you have in you that causes you to want to seek revenge. He knows that this fleshly emotion is not spiritually good for you. The verses above are clear that God will avenge all of the wrongs done on this earth. It is a promise from Him that we, as Believers, must believe and live like it. God tells us to love our enemies. Jesus told God to forgive those who were crucifying him.

God desires us to demonstrate behavior in the Kingdom of God where we love God and serve others. We forgive everyone who has taken advantage of us. We live a totally different kind of life from that of those who live a worldly life. I'll repeat: revenge is a promise from God; He wants you to love your enemies. Start practicing today when you are driving or meeting with others. Your life will be different – complete, full, peaceful, and content.

4. Anger should not be a part of a Believer's life

"You have heard that it was said to the people long ago, 'You shall not murder, and anyone who murders will be subject to judgment.' But I tell you that anyone who is angry with a brother or sister will be subject to judgment." Matthew 5:21-22

It is a bold statement for me to say that anger should not be in any Believer's life. But, I believe that is what Jesus is saying in the verses above. As Believers, we are not to become angry about anything. I don't think any of us can empty ourselves entirely of anger, but I think we all need to spend some time thinking about what provokes us to anger and the possible consequences that can result from our anger.

When and how do you become angry? I ask you to think about the last time the emotion of anger was in your life. Try to recall the circumstances that provoked you to become angry. Anger can come from within yourself because nothing seems to be working the way you expect. You use anger as an outlet for the frustration you may feel. Anger can also be provoked by others...something someone says or does can make you irrationally angry.

God revealed anger several times in my life. One occurrence was as a parent when some neighborhood kids took advantage of my son. I hope I did not scar any of those children's lives with what I said to them. Another incident was as an Assistant coach on a soccer team. My yelling at the kids became so intense during a game that all of the parents and the Head Coach were watching and listening to me instead of the game. I was greatly embarrassed.

The incident that finally changed my life about anger involved my wife. We were living in Florida. It was summer – hot and humid. I was working on my truck and sweating profusely. My wife comes out of the house holding some pink clothing. She apologized but had just washed five brand new dress shirts that I needed for work with something red. They were ruined. I threw some tools into the yard. I yelled at her. I stayed mad at her for several hours. But, the Holy Spirit got my attention by showing me that my relationship with my wife was much more important than five dress shirts. Since that incident, I do not get mad as quickly or as often as I did. I now know that God considers relationships with others more important than any worldly things. Anger has not been completely removed from my life, but I have more peace and joy with my wife and others because I am not quick-tempered or an angry person.

The subject of politics is one that causes anger in many people. In my opinion, there is no politician more valuable than any relationship with your family, friends, or even strangers. When you become angry, your witness for Christ is impaired. You cannot be angry and tell someone about Jesus Christ. They will not listen to you.

How do you remove anger from your life? It is really simple. First of all, I think men are more tempted to be angry than women. This is my opinion. I think men use anger as a crutch to get their way in many situations. We are also more intimidating because of our size and the volume of our voices when we yell. Women get mad too. Whether you are a man or a woman, your anger starts with something small that irritates you. If you do not deal with it right then, it will escalate and you will hear someone say, "you must have gotten up on the wrong side of the bed."

Anger always results in losing control of your mind and emotions. This is why it damages relationships so quickly. When angry, you may use words that you do not normally use. Your facial expressions show anger that is, quite frankly, ugly. You make the other person feel small and insignificant. In the personal incident above, I should have comforted my wife and not made a big deal with her mistake rather than yelling and throwing things. I hope you are beginning to allow the Holy Spirit to reveal incidents of anger in your life and why you became angry. If you would spend the time, after you cool down, to analyze why you became angry, you would begin to get control of one of the worse relationship killers that there are. You must always get to the initial incident that caused you to have some frustration. Stop your feelings right then. You can do this by intentionally conversing with someone about a non-volatile topic. Or, you can make yourself busy at work. Or, you can read a portion from your Bible. Anything that you do should calm your mind and your feelings before you erupt with anger.

One final example that is very personal is that my father used anger to motivate me. As a child, it did not motivate me, but it scared me. Even now in my 60's, if someone starts yelling in my presence, my body has been conditioned to jump. Fathers and Mothers: I beg you not to communicate with your child when you are angry. Children need to be disciplined but not with your loss of control accompanied with yelling and screaming. They need to know what they did wrong, why it was wrong, and then feel the consequences of their wrong.

Every incident with a child should end with that child knowing that you love them unconditionally just like God loves you unconditionally.

I hope what Jesus said in the verses above and these few words that I have written will change your attitude toward anger. I will say it again. I believe that anger should not be present in a true Believer. If you want to justify your anger by using the example of Jesus being angry and overturning the money changing tables in the Tabernacle, then that will have to be between you and God. I do not think you or anyone can justify their anger with that of our Savior and Lord.

During the coming week, think about anger. Look at others that become angry. Find out what causes you to become angry, and then let the Holy Spirit lead you to remove those thoughts from your life. You will experience peace and joy and all of your relationships will be healthy and strong. You are prepared to share Jesus Christ with all others.

5. Believers can do all things

I know what it is to be in need, and I know what it is to have plenty. I have learned the secret of being content in any and every situation, whether well fed or hungry, whether living in plenty or in want. I can do all this through him who gives me strength. Philippians 4:12-13

These verses are frequently referenced to describe the life of a Christian. I thought it would be beneficial to examine them in light of their true meaning to a Christian. The first part of these verses describes what a Christian may have in this world. In either need or in plenty, a Christian is to be content in every situation. In other words, every Christian must reach a state of contentment with no regard as to their condition from a worldly point of view. When a Believer reaches this state of contentment, he/she can move on to the most famous part of these verses, they can do all things through Him (Christ) who gives them strength.

This is speaking about spiritual things – not worldly things. I think this is important, because many Christians misapply this verse to include things that involve their own abilities or inabilities. If I paint a room in my house, I do not need to think that I need Christ to strengthen me to finish the job. I guess I could, but it would seem an awful waste of the strength and power of Christ. If I was planning to spiritually discipline another brother, then I, myself, should be totally weak to the point of dying to self. I must rely totally on the strength that comes from Christ. I cannot have any of my flesh added to the strength that Christ gives me to do something spiritually. It is as if I would be contaminating spiritual power from Christ.

There are two sides to the human flesh, and they are both wrong when applying this verse. I cannot feel confident and strong, and I cannot feel weak and helpless to accomplish spiritual work. I cannot be using my intellect nor can I be lacking in knowledge. I hope you can see that to apply this verse correctly, you must not exist! Your SELF should be totally removed from the incident, and replaced with thoughts of Christ. According to this verse, there is nothing about you that should be allowed in any spiritual activity. Nothing! In Luke 9:23, Jesus said, **"Whoever wants to be my disciple must deny themselves and take up their cross daily and follow me."**

I think this is why we do not see more Believers doing spiritual work with the strength of Christ. They are trying to do it themselves. It is very hard for a human being to give everything up and have the faith that Christ will provide. It is either ALL of Christ or NONE of Christ. Only miraculous spiritual results will occur if you rely on Christ and Christ alone. To Him be all the Glory, and Honor, and Praise!

6. Humility means living your life under God's Authority

So humble yourselves under the mighty hand of God, that he may exalt you in due time. 1 Peter 5:6

Humility is not an action or an attitude. It is a decision to put your life under God's authority in all that you do. The humble person does something for someone else thinking only about the other person. The thought of self is repugnant to humility. Humility is a recurring theme throughout the Bible, because the Lord Jesus was full of humility during his three years of ministry.

Humility is extremely difficult to maintain in the world today. Everything screams for you to make sure you are recognized when something is done. Many people want to make sure their name is included in those who helped with a project; and, it had better be spelled correctly. People who try to act out humility are seen by others as focused on themselves. If you even think that you are humble, it is assured that you are not expressing the humility of our Lord.

Pride is the opposite of humility. Jesus never did anything by putting himself first in a relationship. Jesus never thought of himself and what he was doing. He said that He only did what the Father told him to do. There is no pride or self in that. Jesus placed Himself under the mighty hand of God. As I write this, I think of all the times that I had to hear others say something about what I did. I would not leave it alone. I had to hear one more time something that I said or did that impacted others. That is pure pride with an ugly SELF in control of my life.

Humility requires a submission to all other people. When you meet someone, you are thinking only of him or her and what he or she are saying. Your thoughts are consumed by what that person is going through.

To be a servant of others, God says to place yourself under His authority. Don't think that you know what to do without God's input. In numerous places in the Bible, we are told to sacrifice who we are. Selflessness is a major aspect of a Spirit filled, mature Believer.

Finally, humility is a person being led by God to do the things that give God the glory. In His infinite plan, God uses submission to authority (humility) as a major revelation of who He is to others. It is interesting that there is a reward for forgetting about yourself and being under God's authority – God will exalt you in due time. In other words, God will use your humility to accomplish His will. He will say, "Well done my good and faithful ***servant***."

7. Believers are not grumblers

Do everything without grumbling or arguing, so that you may become blameless and pure, "children of God without fault in a warped and crooked generation." Then you will shine among them like stars in the sky as you hold firmly to the word of life. And then I will be able to boast on the day of Christ that I did not run or labor in vain. Philippians 2:14-16

These are very hard and difficult verses for a Believer to live by. I have always attempted to overlook these verses, especially where it is said to "do everything without grumbling or arguing." Jesus did not grumble or argue. His nature would not allow Him to do those things. I do not know where you would put yourself on a grumble/argue scale, but I know that I would be at the frequent end and Christ would be at the never end.

The world has gotten to a place where others expect you to grumble or argue when things do not go right for you. It is expected that you complain about poor service at a restaurant. It is expected that you demonstrate your dislike for political candidates or your local government. It is expected that you express your displeasure of just about everything that is going on with your job, your company, your community, etc.

I will go even further by saying that you have built into your personality expectations that when they are not met you start to grumble or argue. I challenge you to think about those times of grumbling, and admit to God that your expectations are not realistic for a Believer. After all, the Bible says that Jesus did not even own a pillow to lay His head, but God took care of Him.

The results of not grumbling or arguing are obvious: you will become blameless and pure without fault in a warped and crooked generation. When that happens you will stand out from everyone else as being different. At first, there may be some accusations that you are letting people "run all over you," but that is who we should be as Believers in the world. Someone has to stop the madness. Someone has to bring sanity back into living. Someone has to be at peace when there is anger and fighting everywhere. God has called Christians to be that someone by becoming like Christ.

When you have a Christ-like reaction to what the world throws at you, your opportunities to witness for God increase exponentially. The next time others expect you to grumble about a situation, do the opposite. Look for what can be said as being good and comment on that. Do not give in to the expectations of this world to be spiteful, haughty, or mean.

8. What is the basis of your faith?

The Pharisees came and began to question Jesus. To test him, they asked him for a sign from heaven. He sighed deeply and said, "Why does this generation ask for a miraculous sign? I tell you the truth, no sign will be given to it." Mark 8:11-12

I sincerely believe that our generation has reached a point where Jesus would tell us the same thing that He told the Pharisees in the verses above. "No sign will be given to it." Let me explain why I believe this.

The Pharisees were a group of Jews who were considered the most righteous. The group developed after the Hebrew nation was exiled to Babylon, and the Temple in Jerusalem was destroyed. For all practical purposes, the heart of Judaism had been demolished. All of this happened as a judgment from God because of the Hebrew's repeated disobedience of God's commands.

About 515BC, remnants of the Hebrews returned to Israel and rebuilt the Temple. This is the temple that Jesus walked in and taught in. From all of the judgments from God, the Hebrews finally got the message that they were to be obedient. Therefore, a group developed within the Hebrews to guard against being disobedient to God. This group became known as the Pharisees. They were considered strict righteous living Jews. However, they took being righteous to such an extreme that they slowly grew away from the unconditional love of God and toward a life of being self-righteous by keeping the law. This is the reason that the Pharisees had such a problem with Jesus.

In the verses above, the Pharisees came to Jesus to test him. Jesus had obtained a reputation of being a great teacher and some were saying that He was from God. They asked for a sign from heaven to prove He was who He said He was. This is exactly where most people are today concerning Jesus Christ. "Show me a sign, and I'll believe!"

Did He really exist? Did He really perform all the miracles described in the Bible? Was He really the Son of God? I hope these questions sound familiar because I have talked with so many people about the truth concerning Jesus in the Bible. I believe that most people approach the topic of Christ with only the tool of reason in their mind.

For the Pharisees, they were approaching Christ with the idea that anyone from God would obey all of the Jewish laws, even those not contained in the Old Testament. My point is that they had predetermined the criteria for who Jesus was and had already decided in their hearts that Jesus was not from God. They had a closed mind. This is how a lot of people approach Christianity today. Deep in their mind and in their heart, they will tell God to give them proof that He exists. They have predetermined their answer before discussing the possibility that Jesus is the Son of God.

There are many stories of people who were atheists or agnostics who set out to prove that Jesus was not God. Most of these people became Believers. C. S. Lewis is one of the most famous. Lee Strobel was a staunch doubter who, after extensive research, has now become a strong believer. Note: I recommend reading any of his books but especially, *The Case for Christ.*

The response from Jesus to their request is astounding – he sighed deeply. Take a moment and try to find something in your life that would provoke such a response. I can think of the loss of a football game with only seconds left in the game. The losers would sigh deeply. I can think of parents whose adult child has made another bad decision, and they would sigh deeply. What prompted Jesus to sigh deeply? Jesus was doing only what God was telling Him to do. Yet, the human emotion of sighing deeply was produced, because He knew that true belief does not come from performing a miracle. He knew their belief would not change, because they had preconceived ideas about who He was. It did not matter if He recreated the entire universe in front of them, they would revert back to obeying the law. He was very disappointed that they did not hear and listen to what He was saying about the Kingdom of God.

We are living in a time that "believing" is becoming more and more difficult to base our lives on. But that's exactly what God requires. May I say that if you are waiting on a miracle to substantiate your faith, you will never see a miracle? That is what Jesus told them. This generation, today's generation, is not functioning on faith but rather facts and logic. One person has said, "Give me the facts and I'll believe." With God, it is "Believe and I will show you the facts." What do you base your faith on?

9. Do you respect God?

"You shall not misuse the name of the Lord your God, for the Lord will not hold anyone guiltless who misuses his name. Exodus 20:7

The Almighty is beyond our reach and exalted in power; in his justice and great righteousness, he does not oppress. Therefore, people revere him, for does he not have regard for all the wise in heart?" Job 37:23-24

Then the Lord spoke to Job out of the storm. He said: "Who is this that obscures my plans with words without knowledge? Brace yourself like a man;

I will question you, and you shall answer me. "Where were you when I laid the earth's foundation? Tell me, if you understand. Job 38:1-4

"God Almighty!" Ever heard that used in an inappropriate way. I would say that most of the time this phrase is used in a slang way. "Oh my God!" This is an all too common phrase used by non-Christians and by Believers. It is used to express shock or surprise. It is definitely not used to revere God. "Thank God It's Friday (TGIF)" has been used for years to celebrate the end of a work week. A new TV show has the title, "Thank God It's Thursday!" I am writing about the name of God because all of us are using it too much as a slang phrase with no intention of honoring the Creator of the Universe.

Stop what you are doing and ask yourself, "How do I show genuine respect to God?" This is not a question to be taken lightly. Believers can be lulled into thinking of God as just another person to think about. Of all the people known to man, God deserves our respect. Unfortunately, most of us do not take the time to think on the name of God.

The Bible verses above are clear about respecting the name of God. It should be a daily occurrence that we say, "thank you" to God for what He has done for us. At the very least, we should express our thanks before we say His name in vain. For most of us, we will lose our respect for the name of God as soon as we get into the car to drive somewhere.

I grew up with God's name taken in vain as a common occurrence. There was something that felt like a punch in the stomach when I heard His name spoken in a crude way. I am hoping that many of you reading this feel that same punch indicating a disturbance in your feelings.

Also, the name of Jesus Christ is greatly abused by this world. Most of the time, it's done without the conscious intent of being rebellious. The world and Christians can become desensitized to hearing the Lord's name said in vain. You must not let this happen in your life. God's name is holy. The name of Christ is precious. Please guard your heart and mind from the world's abuse of their names.

I want to make it clear that I am directing all of my comments to you and you alone. I am not suggesting that you correct other people's use of the name of God or Christ. Let us begin with ourselves, as Believers, and make a personal commitment to demonstrate respect for God, Christ, and the Holy Spirit in all that we say and do.

By respecting God in all that you say and do, you will be a "sweet aroma" instead of "rotting flesh" to those people around you (family, friends, and co-workers. You will be amazed at the power of the Holy Spirit to influence others based on your pure and holy behavior.

10. God's promises in your life

This is what I have observed to be good: that it is appropriate for a person to eat, to drink and to find satisfaction in their toilsome labor under the sun during the few days of life God has given them—for this is their lot. [19] Moreover, when God gives someone wealth and possessions, and the ability to enjoy them, to accept their lot and be happy in their toil—this is a gift of God. [20] They seldom reflect on the days of their life, because God keeps them occupied with gladness of heart. Ecclesiastes 5:18-20

The verses above come from the book of Ecclesiastes in the Old Testament. Overall, it is a depressing book written by the wisest man that ever lived, Solomon, David's son. He researched the idea of what makes man happy in this world. He actually experimented with many things himself with the conclusion that happiness cannot be found in the world. If you will read the verses above again, you will note a certain depressed attitude. I want to concentrate on what Solomon has to offer you that will drastically change your attitude toward your personal life.

In verse 18, Solomon identifies three things that are good: eat, drink, and find satisfaction in your labor. He described the labor as most of us would describe it today: "toilsome labor under the sun during the few days of life God has given them—for this is their lot." These words lean toward a negative tone and clearly describes our modern day rat race.

In verse 19, Solomon qualifies the source of "good" wealth as that that comes from God. God also gives you the ability to enjoy them. This would not be the case for most wealthy people today, because, instead of enjoying it, they consume it on themselves in extravagant and vulgar ways. Solomon was one of the richest men in the world. He calls all of the gifts regarding wealth as gifts from God. Again, extremely few wealthy people look at wealth as a gift from God.

Verse 20 is for you. If you can understand its impact and apply it to your life, your attitude will change greatly. He is continuing to talk about rich people who treat their wealth and possessions as a gift from God. I hope you can see that Solomon hasn't been talking about rich people as we define them. He is talking about you and me and anyone who views their wealth and possessions as gifts from God. If you do, God provides the most wonderful gift of all that impacts our entire lives. God's promise is that He will keep them occupied with gladness of heart. This is so good.

Another way of saying "They seldom reflect on the days of their life" is to say that they don't worry about their wealth and possessions, their families, what the future may look like, and all the other things that occupy a person's mind that is not Godly. One big issue is when something eventful happens in your life (bad or good), your mind will be distracted by that topic for years. For example, something in high school or college that was a success or a failure could occupy your mind in a negative way. Other examples are a divorce; loss of a loved one; bankruptcy; foreclosure on your home, loss of job; and, many more.

God is giving you the key to peace and contentment on this earth: believe that everything you have and own is a gift from God. Instead of being in bondage to anything in your past life, God will keep you occupied with greatness of heart. Praise the Lord! Basically, if you are always living in the past, I don't see how you can know God's plan for you in the future. This is just like driving a boat by watching its wake. Try God's plan for removing those things in the past.

This is a spiritual truth that could be new to you. If it is, I suggest you do a complete heart and mind motivated evaluation of everything you own. You must get a clean conscience from the Holy Spirit before God's promise becomes effective.

11. When Christians stop witnessing, God judges

And the Word of God says,

When the men got up to leave, they looked down toward Sodom, and Abraham walked along with them to see them on their way. Then the LORD said, "Shall I hide from Abraham what I am about to do? Genesis 18:16-17

The setting for the above Bible passage is the visit of three men to Abraham and Sarah. You can discover later in the story that two of the men are angels and the third is God or the pre-incarnate Jesus Christ. No one has ever seen God; therefore, I conclude that this is Jesus Christ appearing on earth. This happens numerous times in the Old Testament.

We have something recorded here that God is saying to Himself, "Should I hide something from Abraham?" What was He going to do? Destroy Sodom and Gomorrah? I agree that is the ultimate objective, but I want you to look at it a little differently. He is planning to destroy them, but first He is going to "judge" Sodom and Gomorrah. That is important when you start reading the dialogue that Abraham will have with God.

Guess who is living over in Sodom and Gomorrah at the time of this visit by God: Abraham's nephew, Lot. The salient question about Lot is Abraham's concept of how God will judge. The destroying of Sodom and Gomorrah is carrying out God's judgment. You can see Abraham's concern about God's judgment. Every one of you has to deal with the concept of God's judgment. Is there a just God? Can I believe that God will judge this earth fairly and justly? Even if I disagree, do I believe God is just? There are some things that God does (or is going to do) that you will say, "I don't believe in a God that can include small children in His judgment." This is the point where your faith tells you that God is a just God.

I have heard it said that if God does not destroy America soon, He would need to apologize to Sodom and Gomorrah. This business about judging Sodom and Gomorrah and looking to see if it is worthy of being saved from judgment prompts many people to draw parallels to America, today. As Abraham argues on behalf of Sodom and Gomorrah, we (Christians) are the ones standing against God executing His judgment on America.

God is in the business of judging. He's in the business of saving and having relationships, but only after so long, He says, "I have given them all the chances in the world to have that relationship with me. I must judge them." This is true for all nations as well as every single individual.

The only thing holding God's judgment back as we live today is the witness and testimony of Christians as empowered by the Holy Spirit. God does not want anyone to perish. However, when Christians stop witnessing to others, God may say, "It is time to judge!"

12. Love one another

And this is my prayer: that your love may abound more and more in knowledge and depth of insight, so that you may be able to discern what is best and may be pure and blameless for the day of Christ, filled with the fruit of righteousness that comes through Jesus Christ—to the glory and praise of God. Philippians 1:9-11

As you read the verses above, you can see that Paul (writer of Philippians) was saying a prayer for the Christians in Philippi. The first thing he prayed about was their love for one another. A Believer's love for other Believers should always be increasing. The word "love" in these verses is the same Greek word for "love" in the well-known John 3:16 verse, "For God so loved the world." The Greek word "agape" is translated as unconditional love. I wish all translations of the Bible would put this word in parentheses wherever in occurs. Someone who studies the Bible would know that whenever the word is used in the Bible, it is intended to mean the highest form of any thoughts that you may have about love.

God used agape love to describe His attitude toward sinners. Everyone who believes Christ died on the cross to obtain God's forgiveness for our sins has experienced God's love. This "love" is not an emotion; rather, it is a decision that God and Christ made for all mankind. This "love" implies a sacrifice meaning that the one who shows this kind of love is putting others first. Jesus expressed this kind of love when He sacrificed Himself for you, me, and all mankind.

Christian love is present when the love of God is in our minds. Because He first loved us, we must love one another (1 John 4:19). Christian love is not prompted by feelings. You don't have to and you should not wonder if you feel love for another Christian. As a matter of fact, Christians should be careful to distinguish between their emotional love and agape love. You don't wait to feel like serving others. It is a conscious and deliberate decision that you make as a Christian. Many times your flesh will rise up within you and give you reasons not to serve others. When you are consumed by self-thinking (flesh), you cannot have an attitude of Christian love. Christian love is always identifying and serving the needs of others; regardless of who they are or their relationship with you.

Paul goes on to identify results when we express Christian love. He says that our thoughts about Christian love should reflect an increase in knowledge and depth of insight. He also uses the word discernment. In Christianity today, there is not an emphasis on increasing in discernment as part of our spiritual growth. Agape love is discussed, but not in the context that you will increase in spiritual discernment of others. In my opinion, this topic should be a routine part of discussions among Christians. When you grasp the concept of Christian love and apply it in a practical way as you live your life, you will begin to see what is best, pure, and blameless. In other words, your obedience to the commands of Christ comes from your depth of insight and discernment brought on by your application of Christian love to other Christians.

Spiritual discernment was a character trait of Jesus Christ during His ministry on earth. Read John, Chapters 3 and 4, and you will see spiritual discernment by Jesus: the stories of Nicodemus and the Samaritan woman at the well. You will increase in your spiritual discernment when you increase your agape love for other Christians. When Christians do not display agape love to other Christians, those people without Christ can easily accuse us of being just like the world. Worldly love does not and cannot include agape love.

Finally, Paul says that when you have removed self-thinking and replaced it with agape love, you are filled with the fruit of righteousness that comes through Jesus Christ. This is an amazing statement that every Christian should understand. Paul is saying that not only can you be as righteous as Christ, but he also says that, as a Believer, you are filled with the righteousness of Christ. Your mind can only understand this from a spiritual perspective.

Think again of the love of God and Christ for Christ to willingly and innocently die as payment for the penalty of our sins (eternal death), and for us to be forgiven of all of our sins. His sacrifice enables us to experience eternal life with God. I hope you can see the strong connection between God's expression of agape love through the crucifixion of Christ, and your attitude of agape love toward others.

Consider the event of Jesus in the Garden praying to His father, "not my will, but your will be done" (read John, Chapter 17). At the same time, consider the agape love that other Christians have shown you. This is a potentially dangerous thought, because the majority of Christians express love for others based on a list of conditions that they have created. When this happens, it is easy to think, "If they love me, then I'll love them." This is worldly love and not agape love. Worldly love always includes certain conditions or requirements for loving others. Thankfully, Christ did not think that way when He was crucified;

otherwise, He would not have allowed himself to be crucified, and we could not have forgiveness of sins.

I encourage you to frequently and intentionally meditate on this word "love". You will experience spiritual growth in your discernment as well as becoming more Christ-like. You will definitely experience some major changes in your life in your relationship with others.

But love your enemies, do good to them, and lend to them without expecting to get anything back. Then your reward will be great, and you will be children of the Most High, because he is kind to the ungrateful and wicked. Luke 6:35

Of all the Bible passages, this is one that we would all agree should be removed from the Holy Scriptures. Or, maybe not! When God put it in His Word, He must have had a good reason to make such outlandish claims. As a sense of balance of judgment, this passage sends the needle way past the rule that says to be nice to your enemies. This is one command where Jesus makes it clear that, as a Believer, your behavior is to be dramatically different from others in the world.

Enemies occur in our neighborhoods with fence lines, HOAs, and yard maintenance. Enemies occur in our stores when someone breaks in line or you cannot find anyone to help you. Enemies pop up when it is time to settle a bill that is higher than quoted or additional work was done that you did not authorize. Enemies confront us when we work with good ethics and they do not (e.g., inflated travel expenses). There are so many opportunities that illustrate the values of the kingdom of this world versus the kingdom of God.

In the above passage, Jesus is asking His Believers to live the values of the Kingdom of God. First of all, you should love your enemies. The Greek word for love in this passage is not the one I had hoped it would be. This word love means the God-like love between God and man. In other words, self-sacrificing love that can only be provided by the Holy Spirit. This really hits home with the significant difference of how we are to love others. We are to love them as God loves them. This seems almost impossible from a worldly perspective. But our God says to love (agape) our enemies. He gives an illustration of lending to your enemies and not to expect to get anything in return. Wow! That is hard to do. But, that is God's expectation for His followers. We are to be different.

He does share that your reward will be great, and you will be God's children. That sounds pretty good to me. He goes on to say that God is kind to the ungrateful and wicked. That is not my reaction to those kinds of people. I want to retaliate, but God has a different set of values for His Kingdom. We need to learn what they are and live by them. The world will be a different place to live our lives.

In this is love brought to perfection among us, that we have confidence on the day of judgment because as he is, so are we in this world. There is no fear in love, but perfect love drives out fear because fear has to do with punishment, and so one who fears is not yet perfect in love. 1 John 4:17-18

The book of First John is more of a sermon than a letter like the other books in the New Testament. John was the pastor of the church at Ephesus, and First John is a sermon that he gave the Believers of that church. The purpose of the sermon was to discuss the high standards that a Believer should live by in the world. Compromise was beginning to enter into the church similar to what is happening in many churches today. God intends the church (made up of Believers) to be different from this world. To take on some of the characteristics of worldliness was to move away from God. As you read this chapter, ask the Holy Spirit if there are any areas in your life where the love of Christ cannot be found. At the same time, celebrate your life in Christ when you are found to be like Christ.

"Love" is the major theme of the above Bible verses. John presents love as something that Believers increasingly mature in and apply to their lives. As Believers, we should have the goal to make the love of God complete in our lives.

God's love is always defined by a decision. Love in the world is usually described with emotions or sexual overtones. I can love my brothers in this world because of the closeness of growing up together. That is not God's love. If one of my brothers does something that endangers our relationship, I probably will not feel like loving him. But, if he was in need, then I could decide to ignore the problems and help to satisfy his need.

The same type of decision is made when we do something for others that do not deserve anything from us. They could be considered as our enemy, but God would say to love your enemies. The use of the word in that context is to decide to put aside any animosity or ill feelings and to help them, especially if it requires a sacrifice on our part. Christ sacrificed himself for the forgiveness of our sins and the restoration of a healthy relationship with God.

I think as Christians we need to clearly distinguish that we are to love others in the form of decisions we make. When we learn to do this on a regular basis, we are growing to be more Christ-like in our attitude and behavior. God says that we will not fear the Day of Judgment, because we decided to love our enemies as Christ did.

"As He is, so are we in this world" is a strong statement to make about the sinful human being. This is only possible as we decide to love others unconditionally. As the Christ love grows in us it will be perfected to the point of experiencing no fear in this world. Realize that God loves (has decided to love) you as you are. Take a moment of each day to realize that God's love is His decision and is not based on your behavior. Thank you Lord for loving us so that we can have boldness and confidence in our living relationship with you.

This is how love is made complete among us so that we will have confidence on the Day of Judgment: in this world we are like Jesus. There is no fear in love. But perfect love drives out fear, because fear has to do with punishment. The one who fears is not made perfect in love. 1 John 4:17-18

A child who is abused would have a difficult time learning, even as an adult, what love is. Fear can damage a child for a lifetime. Fear can affect every future relationship for a child. Fear will probably have a negative impact on their relationship with their spouse and children. It will damage relationships with other relatives and friends. Fear causes significant damage to the mental health of a child. It is not impossible, but it is made more difficult for an abused child to show love to others when they are adults.

This discussion about abused children can be applied to adults. God considers us as "his children". Many times in the Bible, Believers are referred to as the children of God. In Romans 5:18, the term "Abba Father" is the same as our calling on God by saying, "Daddy." As adults, we experience so many negative events in our lifetime that our minds and emotions are damaged. We cannot maintain healthy relationships, because of the fear of being hurt again and again. This is the fear that results when the things of this world pile up on us. Satan, who currently has dominion on this earth, has used fear as his major tactic to cause Believers to neglect the love of God.

The verses above direct our attention not to this world, but to the kingdom of God. One day, God will judge all of earth. As Believers, we do not have to fear that judgment, because we are like Christ. Knowing the love He shared by dying on the cross, allows Believers to love and live without fear. There is no fear in love. In fact, perfect love (God's unconditional love) drives out all of our fear. As Believers, we all probably need to work on making this truth a reality in our lives on this earth.

Not only do we not have to fear God's judgment, but also we can live on this earth with confidence. The Oxford Dictionary defines confidence as follows: "the feeling or belief that one can rely on someone or something; firm trust." By relying on God and focusing on His love for us as Believers, this world cannot present anything to us that should cause us to fear.

Please think about what you are worrying about or fearful of happening. Your next thought should be, "I do not have to fear anything on this earth, because God loves me unconditionally." If you do continue to possess fear in your life, then you do not trust that you are like Jesus. You have given Satan an opportunity to negatively impact all of your relationships. This is an Absolute Truth about living life on earth. God encourages Believers to have strong and healthy relationships with Him and others. Allow the perfect love of God to consume your every thought and action. Do not be afraid of anything on this earth. As a child of God, you have no basis for being fearful.

13. Obedience and Disobedience

The name of the righteous is used in blessings, but the name of the wicked will rot. Proverbs 10:7

If you look back over your life (regardless of your current age – young or old), God will show you the spiritual impact you have had on others. He may show you someone that you had the opportunity to present the story of the gospel, and they accepted Jesus Christ by faith. You may have encouraged someone in their spiritual living to "be strong and of good courage" in their faith and belief. You may have given someone a spiritual truth from the Bible that they needed to get through some tough times here on earth. They could not have done it without you. You may have anonymously given financial aid that helped someone get out of the bondage of debt and become free to live a life for God. Because of your obedience to God, their life changed, and they now live a life for God. There are many more examples where Christians have helped others with a pure and clean heart. Their obedience was proved by their actions.

All of these spiritual events are considered as "acts of kindness to others". They are also called "self-sacrifice" for the benefit of others. They are the result of a spiritual interaction between a Christian and the Holy Spirit whereby God, through the Holy Spirit, has given you a clear picture of the will of God in serving others. You respond in obedience to God. Every time you, as a Christian, act in obedience to God, the verse above says that your name is considered righteous and results in a blessing to others. I have experienced this several times when I hear certain names mentioned that gave me an immediate blessing and renewed strength to live a life for God. Those names were of Christians who were strong in their faith. They were at peace with this world. They never seemed to be controlled by other people. In fact, even though they were always in the background, they were heavily involved in serving others. They truly lived a full and abundant life.

The verse above contains a very strong positive outcome for obedience. However, it is not the same when disobedience is in our lives. None of us like to read the rest of the verse. Your disobedience to God becomes wickedness and your name will produce rot. These are very strong words and no one wants to hear them.

As human beings, we naturally want to avoid things that hurt. At the same time, I realize that God wants you and me pure and clean before Him. Pondering on this verse and the significant impact it had on my life caused me to stop and ask God to always put me through a review of my obedience or lack of obedience to Him no matter how much pain was involved. I want to be pure, clean, and holy before Him, and I can only do that if I love Him with all my heart, mind, soul, and strength...AND, if I love others as I love myself. A large part of my obedience to God is seen through my serving others.

Try to think of situations that you have found yourself in that were clearly either a testimony for God or a weakness of your flesh that results in sin taking control of your life. The memories of those situations will either be the favorable aroma of a sweet smelling flower, or, if your decision was to live for your flesh, then the aroma is more like a stench of something rotting.

How do you think of your disobedience to God today? Have you decided that there are small disobediences that you can get by with God? Does the impact you have on others become a huge part of your view of disobeying God? Jesus summarized the obedience to God as loving Him and serving others. How do you think you are doing in showing God's self-sacrificial love to others? Jump off the pedestal you have built for yourself to make you feel good about yourself. Ask God to put you through a review of your obedience to Him by using the verse above. Ask Him to do this on a regular basis. Ask His forgiveness now (as you read this), and start looking at others as better than yourself.

14. Do not grow weary; God's love endures forever

Let us not become weary in doing good, for at the proper time we will reap a harvest if we do not give up. Galatians 6:9 (NIV)

Let us not grow tired of doing good, for in due time we shall reap our harvest, if we do not give up. Galatians 6:9 (NABRE)

"I am tired, worn out, weary, wasted, with no energy. How much longer can I go on?" These words occur in everyone's life. If we are doing a repetitive action (e.g., going to work), a lack of endurance could be a part of your life. If you are going through an illness, the discomfort and pain could be so unbearable that you do not think you could survive. When you are caring for sick children, a seriously ill spouse, or aging parents (or all of them at once), it is very easy to ask God, "How much longer?" To "endure to the end" is a difficult task for Christians, but that is what God is asking each of us to do.

There is an interesting perspective to the beatings that Christ suffered before He died on the cross and the pain ended. This is difficult to comprehend, but God could not allow Jesus to die while He was suffering through a horrendous beating. I would go so far as to say that no matter how long or how harsh the beatings were Jesus had to endure to the end so that He would be crucified (see Psalm 22). Paul said this about his own sufferings, **"We were under great pressure, far beyond our ability to endure, so that we despaired of life itself."** (2 Corinthians 1:8)

There are several things in the Bible that will endure to the end such as: God's Kingdom; God's faithfulness; God's righteousness; the Word of the Lord; and, finally and most predominantly, is "His love endures forever." Those four words give me so much relief from my own problems. I hope they do yours.

Endurance requires inward strength of the individual. It requires the thinking that everything will come to an end. A person needs spiritual strength, stamina, and trust in the love of the Lord that endures forever. Finally, we need to be encouraging one another. A visit to the hospital, a card received in the mail, food taken to a home, phone calls that say, "I love you as God loves you." Every Christian should not let a week go by without fulfilling their Godly responsibility to be involved with someone else who is "enduring" hardships.

"Therefore, brothers and sisters, in all our distress and persecution we were encouraged about you because of your faith. For now we really live, since you are standing firm in the Lord." (1 Thessalonians 3:7-8) We should do this encouraging while we ourselves are trying to endure. Only then will we be accomplishing God's will and acknowledging to everyone that God's "love endures forever."

15. Pride is the sin of all sins

When pride comes, then comes disgrace, but with humility comes wisdom. Pride goes before destruction, a haughty spirit before a fall. Proverbs 11:2; 16:18

For everything in the world—the lust of the flesh, the lust of the eyes, and the pride of life—comes not from the Father but from the world. 1 John 2:16

"My Father God! I have sinned against you and other people. I have allowed pride to come into my life and damage my relationship with you and others. I acknowledge the sin of pride to you, and I know that you have forgiven me. You have cleansed me through the blood of Christ and have forgotten my sin. I praise you and thank you with a grateful heart. Amen."

This is a common prayer for my life. God has done so many things with my life through the power of the Holy Spirit that it is a temptation to take pride in what I do. Regretfully, I allow my flesh to begin to think, "Look what I did!" When I do this sin is conceived in my heart and my words, thoughts, and actions negatively impact others. This is not what I want to happen. I constantly remind myself that only the Holy Spirit can work in my life to do good things. Pride borders on blasphemy when you take personal credit for good works rather than giving praise to God. This is why I titled this chapter, "Pride: The Sin of All Sins.

The sin of pride in a Believer's life is difficult to identify. Of all sins, pride is the hardest to identify in yourself and the easiest for others to see in you. The flesh will not allow a person to say, "I have the sin of pride." Only the Holy Spirit can show a Believer pride in their life. You must reach a point where you live by this spiritual Truth in your life on a daily basis.

The Holy Spirit will reveal the sin of pride in the life of a Believer through the impact that pride has on others. Think about some people in whom you can see pride. Look at how they impact you and others. They are people that you do not want to be around, because you feel inadequate. In other words, pride in a Believer can be demeaning to another Believer. It has a more damaging impact on non-Believers (that is why you hear the church is full of hypocrites – "the pride of life.") Prideful people will negatively impact another person's self-esteem. Prideful people usually do most of the talking in a conversation. Pride can take the form of thinking that you are better than others. Any and every discussion will be about something that the prideful person has done. This is where I am most guilty. Pride can destroy relationships if not removed from the Believer.

In the verses above, pride produces disgrace, destruction, and a fall. Pride can take control of a person to the point that it is extremely difficult for that person to recognize pride in their attitude. Pride manifests itself in you wanting your own way of doing things. A serious pride problem will cause you to become angry when you do not get your way. This is when relationships are damaged. I would say that pride is the most common cause of relationship problems.

All Believers must guard their hearts and minds about thinking too much of themselves. You can see from the verses above that pride comes from the world. We become so enamored with something that we excel in that we allow our flesh to feel good. This is the first step toward giving into pride. If not nipped in the bud, pride will slowly take over a Believer's life and become a stronghold of sin.

As a Believer, you must ask God to identify pride in your life. When you ask God, you must be in a position of self-denial. I suggest you picture in your mind standing at the foot of the cross and hearing Jesus say, **"Father, forgive them, for they do not know what they are doing."** (Luke 23:34) You must reach a point of humility about yourself before the Holy Spirit can show you the pride in your life. You will not feel good when this happens. Remember that it is the flesh in you that will not feel good. The new spiritual creation that you are with God will reach a point of peace that cannot be defined in worldly terms. You will see God working in your life. You will also begin to see the needs of others. Your focus will move off yourself and onto God and others. This is a Christ-like attitude that all Believers should have.

Pride is always thinking about itself. It does not allow the person to think about God or others. This violates the two commands that Jesus gave that summarize all of the commands of God: "love God with all your heart, soul, and mind, and love others as yourself." If a Believer does not repent and confess the sin of pride, then it is impossible to have a strong spiritual relationship with God.

There are times that pride is an acceptable attitude to have. In Proverbs, pride is used to describe the emotion that grandparents have for their grandchildren. The context is that how to live a spiritual life was passed along from their children to their grandchildren. Many times in the letters that Paul wrote, he says that he takes pride in the spiritual growth of others. I hope you can see that this kind of pride concerns spiritual matters. It is impossible to see spiritual things when you are thinking only of yourself.

Take the time to ask God to identify any and all pride in your life. Jesus said that if anyone desires to follow Him, he must deny himself on a daily basis. Do you tell God that you deny yourself each day of your life? Have you prayed something similar to my prayer at the beginning of this chapter? Allow the Holy Spirit to reveal where pride occurs in your life. Now is the time to identify and repent of the sin of pride in your life. By doing this, your life will never be the same.

16. God will rescue you

He reached down from on high and took hold of me; he drew me out of deep waters. He rescued me from my powerful enemy, from my foes, who were too strong for me. They confronted me in the day of my disaster, but the Lord was my support. He brought me out into a spacious place; he rescued me because he delighted in me. Psalm 18:16-19

There are so many things in this world that cause fear, uncertainty, and doubt. The things of this world may seem to be totally out of control. You may feel closed in or about to go under for the third time, but you have a rescuer – God!

Human beings are the only living creatures that desire to intentionally hurt other human beings. These people empty themselves of any and all concern for others. Life is meaningless to them. These kinds of things bother us, because God puts life as His most valuable creation.

We can also suffer through relationship problems that can be a constant worry for us. We can make some bad financial decisions that keep us up at night worrying about how to get out of a deep, dark hole that looks too deep. Physical illnesses can suck the life out of you whether it is you that is sick or a loved one. These problems can overwhelm you to the point of physical and mental illness. You will feel heavy and drained of energy. You may not be able to see a solution and your attitude will be of despair and hopelessness.

The Bible verses above gives you relief from any of the problems that you may be going through. Psalm 18 was written when David was being hunted and persecuted. Things were looking hopeless against overwhelming odds. I am sure that David felt weak and helpless. We can have the same feelings of despair that David suffered. But David had a rescuer just like you have.

God reaches from the spiritual realm to put His protective power around you in the worldly realm. He does not say that He will remove the problems. God says He will rescue you from things that are totally out of your control. He will turn your hopelessness into a greater and brighter hope. He will be with you throughout any problem that you may have. The question is whether you believe God's Word or not.

Let me repeat, "Do you believe God's word?" This takes faith, because without faith it is impossible to please God. God is saying to get your mind off your problems and to guard your heart. Rest in the Word of God that is more powerful than any other force known to man. He will rescue you and support you. He will delight in you. He is the all powerful and all mighty Creator who loves you unconditionally. With these thoughts, God will appear much more awesome and comforting than any problems you may have. But you must think on His Greatness and not your small, temporary problems.

17. Maintain your relationship to always be near God

Come near to God and he will come near to you. Wash your hands, you sinners, and purify your hearts, you double-minded. James 4:8

Many of you have felt the longing to be near someone when separated by long distances. More times than I like, I had to be separated from my family for business reasons. These separations ranged from a few days to 3 months. I really did not like it. God desperately desires to have a strong and personal relationship with you, where the distance between you and God becomes shorter and shorter. God has placed inside all of us the desire to be close to Him. He has and will do anything to bring you closer to Him. It stands to reason that, as Believers, we should have the longing to be near God. However, that longing does not occur in the life of many Believers. Why?

Worldly distractions are major culprits for coming between you and God. God knows that we are very weak in this area, and He will set in motion activities that will bring us back to Him. Be open to the Holy Spirit to show you these activities or even people whose purpose it is to encourage you to grow closer to Him. With worldly desires so tempting, it is too easy to quench the desire in your heart to come near to God. Take an inventory of the desires in your heart to see if you truly long for a relationship with God or with the things of this world.

As a personal example, early in my life, I was totally and completely distracted from God by football. On one Sunday, this obsessive desire to watch football came back to me as a wake-up call. I had left church early to catch the pre-game football shows. When my wife and two children came home, my seven-year-old son told me that he had accepted Jesus Christ as his Savior while riding home in the car with his mother. At that moment, I felt I was so far away from my family and God. My selfish desires had destroyed an opportunity to see God at work in my own son's life. I realized that my son was a whole lot closer to God than I was. I was ashamed. God used that event to bring me closer to Him.

Another way you can grow further away from God is through the development of bad habits. An example of a bad habit is the gradual withdrawal from attending church and Bible Study classes. Instead of looking on these activities as moving closer to God, you begin to look at your fleshly desires and try to satisfy those. Sunday mornings can become a bad habit without church. Your Sunday morning may go something like this: get up and make a cup of coffee; go outside to get the newspaper; read it from cover to cover; look up at the clock, and it is too late to go to church. Your relationship with God just took a big hit.

Another pulling away from God is when you do not want to become involved with other Believers. If you do not have fellowship with other Christians, it is almost a guarantee that any longing for God will slowly disappear. There is a philosophy in the world defined as "you leave me alone and I'll leave you alone." Regular fellowship with other Believers will always bring you closer to God.

Since you are a Believer, YOU have been brought near to God because of Christ. YOU are now NEAR GOD!! Now that you are near to God, you can have a personal and intimate relationship with the Creator and Sustainer of all of life. AMAZING!!!

18. All of our sins are removed by the blood of Christ

For the life of a creature is in the blood, and I have given it to you to make atonement for yourselves on the altar; it is the blood that makes atonement for one's life. Leviticus 17:11

Therefore, brothers and sisters, since we have confidence to enter the Most Holy Place by the blood of Jesus... Hebrews 10:19

But if we walk in the light, as he is in the light, we have fellowship with one another, and the blood of Jesus, his Son, purifies us from all sin. 1 John 1:7

After Christ died on the cross, He took some of His blood to the perfect altar in heaven. When He sprinkled His blood on that altar, all of our sins were forgiven. God would no longer see our sins but only the blood of Christ that purifies us from all sin. This is God's plan for removing sin and guilt from us so that we can enter into the presence of a holy God. (See Hebrews 7 – 10)

After Adam and Eve sinned in the Garden of Eden, they tried to cover up their sin with fig leaves. God declared it inadequate, so He made garments out of the skins of animals (blood sacrifice) to cover up their sins (Genesis 3:20).

God's plan to remove sin continued to be revealed throughout the Old Testament. This was done through an animal sacrifice on an altar. God showed humanity how to build a tabernacle patterned after the one in heaven. After this temporary tabernacle was finished, God instituted an annual sacrifice to remove the sins of the people. However, this ritual had to be repeated every year. With Christ, He died and presented His blood to the perfect altar in heaven one time for all past, present, future sins of every human being.

It is through the sacrifice of an innocent man (Jesus Christ) that will allow you to face a holy God. The blood of Christ has made atonement for your sins once and for all. Knowing this, we can enter the Most Holy Place with confidence because we will not be carrying any of our sins with us. The blood of Christ has purified us from all sin.

I hope this gives you a huge jolt to your belief in what Christ did for you on the cross. I hope it also gives you a more meaningful understanding of the love of the Father (John 3:16). Any thought of our sins takes us away from realizing God's love for us. Our sins should never occupy our minds. God has taken care of our sins. Instead, our thoughts should be on the unconditional love of God, and Christ who demonstrates that love while we are sinners.

19. Spiritual battles are being waged all around you

Do not fret because of those who are evil or be envious of those who do wrong; for like the grass they will soon wither, like green plants they will soon die away. Trust in the Lord and do good; dwell in the land and enjoy safe pasture. Take delight in the Lord, and he will give you the desires of your heart. Commit your way to the Lord; trust in him and he will do this: He will make your righteous reward shine like the dawn, your vindication like the noonday sun. Be still before the Lord and wait patiently for him;
Psalm 37:1-7

Jesus faced spiritual battles during His entire ministry. It is good to be reminded that there are spiritual battles being waged all around us. Sometimes they will include us directly. As Believers, we need to know God's perspective on the evildoers. He says not to fret or be envious. Do not let their behavior influence your behavior toward others. Otherwise, you will succumb to the same evil attitudes that confronted you. God also reminds us that they do not hang around very long; so, you do not have to put up with them but only for a short time. That is very welcome news.

God says to trust Him and He will give you the desires of your heart. These desires are not your wants. These are the deep down life-giving ideas that roll around in your head as something that is just not possible. With God nothing is impossible. God places great value on committing your way to Him. In other words, each day belongs to God to do with you as He pleases as you allow Him. Allowing Him is where we will most likely see the greatest miracles He performs in our lives. Take delight in the Lord and all that He does. Be aware of His works in this world now and in the past. Your righteousness will shine before others like you have never seen before. You will truly be on the edge of a spiritual mystical union with the God of Creation.

20. Thankfulness should be a permanent attitude for all Believers

Shout for joy to the Lord, all the earth. Worship the Lord with gladness; come before him with joyful songs. Know that the Lord is God. It is he who made us, and we are his; we are his people, the sheep of his pasture. Enter his gates with thanksgiving and his courts with praise; give thanks to him and praise his name. For the Lord is good and his love endures forever; his faithfulness continues through all generations. Psalm 100:1-5

This is the entire Psalm 100 and it is full of rich thoughts that should be in the minds of Believers. I propose to you that if you would read this Psalm everyday for a month, your attitude will change. You will have a more positive outlook on life. Your problems will still be there, but there will be lightness in your heart. God could use any part of this Psalm to bring you to a closer relationship to Him. If you would allow the Holy Spirit to bring to your mind a thought, or a phrase, or just one single word from this Psalm that would become a part of you, you will experience some of the abundant life that Jesus said we could have in the here and now.

The Psalm begins with a "shout" meaning that you don't start with a whisper or a soft voice. This is something great, and God wants you to shout for joy. The only way you can sincerely shout is by putting yourself in the presence of God and realizing his Glory. Shout! Unfortunately, the best worldly example is hearing people at sporting events. There is always a lot of shouting going on. The reason why is there is a motivation in their heart to voice support for their team.

Do you support God and everything He is doing for you? If you do then you will "worship the Lord with gladness and come before Him with joyful songs". I hope you can see already that this Psalm is like the greatest Encourager you could possibly have in your life. All of us have our favorite songs that we can sing to ourselves. Mine is "Heaven came down and glory filled my soul." It is a song that once I heard it, it became one of those things that you cannot get out of your head. I am glad because the Holy Spirit reminds me to sing it at various times when my soul is in need of the Presence of God.

The Psalm continues with an affirmation that God is GOD. He has made you and you are one of His people. You are a Believer! You are a child of the King of the Universes. You are a co-heir with Christ for everything that God will give you. You have received eternal life and a guarantee (Holy Spirit) that you will live with God for eternity. These are the kinds of thoughts, phrases, or words that I am suggesting become part of you. As you are reading this, if the Holy Spirit nudges your soul over something, write it down and put it some place where you will see it for two or three days. It will become part of your life, and, Praise the Lord, it will replace something that the world had put into your life that God wanted to remove from you.

When we go to church to meet and greet other Believers, the Psalm says to enter with a heart of thanksgiving and the thought of praise in our minds. On the way to church, spend time thinking about the past week and acknowledging sincere thanks to God for the things that happen – both good and bad. God had a purpose in your life for the week and He is always working on you. Be thankful that He is faithful. Praise Him for the work He will do in your life for the coming week.

The Lord is good and His Name is to be praised. What is His name? He has many names identified in the Bible. You can do a Google search for the names of God and you will probably be very surprised at how many different names God has. Search for one that has meaning in your life. I love His holy name of "I Am". That name of God is all-inclusive. There is nothing outside of God. When I get despondent over the conditions of the world, I think of "I Am", and everything comes back to a constant. God is over all. He has left nothing undone. His purposes and plans are solid and complete. There really is nothing else to think about when I think of the "I Am" of everything that could ever be known. That thought is so comforting to me. This is an example of what I mean when I say to allow the Holy Spirit to reveal to you a thought, a phrase or a word that you can ponder, consider, dwell on during the week.

Finally, his faithfulness continues through all generations. He never changes. There was a point in my life when I realized that there is no human being that can always be faithful. It is part of our sin nature. All of us are so far from being called "faithful". If you think you are exempt from this, consider your faithfulness to God. I believe all of us can recall times when we were not faithful to God. Now, contrast that with God who is always faithful. Your confidence in the Lord and the peace that you sense that there is one thing in all of your life that you can always call faithful – GOD.

Thankfulness for who God is should be a permanent attitude of all Believers. This can be true for you by dwelling on something about God for a week or two. Make it a spiritual exercise to always have a thought or a word that keeps coming to your mind. This will bring on life-changing attitudes in your life and you will experience God like you never have before.

21. Meditate on God's Word to learn of Him

I meditate on your precepts and consider your ways. I delight in your decrees; I will not neglect your word. Psalm 119:15-16

Psalm 119 is the longest chapter in the Bible. It takes a few days to read all of it; at least, it does for me. The primary purpose of Psalm 119 is to talk about your relationship with God by thinking about His nature. You can learn about His value system; about His ethics; and, the way He goes about judging. If you find some verses difficult to understand, keep on reading. If, however, you, as a Christian, do not take the time to read and study the Bible, how will you ever know more about God and His extreme desire to have a personal relationship with you?

The verse above is an encouragement for you to start reading and studying God's Word. There are four key phrases: (1) meditate on your precepts, (2) consider your ways, (3) delight in your decrees, and, (4) do not neglect your word. I will discuss the first two this week and the second two next week.

a. **Meditate on your precepts:** Meditate is something everyone does but is not aware of it. Meditation as a religious act has been heavily applied to Eastern religions. This has kept many Christians from meditating. However, meditation is something that God clearly desires of you, as a Christian. Meditation is NOT an emptying of your mind but rather an intense focus on something. In the verse above, the focus is to be on God's precepts. A precept is a "commandment" usually regarding moral conduct. As soon as I say "moral conduct," we Christians have a lot of work to do. When you meditate on God's precepts, you are focusing on why God has His commandments and what they have to do with who He is.

b. **Consider your ways:** I love the word "consider." It lets me look at something from several different perspectives to arrive at a conclusion. In this case, we have to consider God's ways. When Jesus was confronted with the prostitute caught in the act, consider how He redirected the attention of her accusers to themselves. Similar to this situation is when someone is speaking badly about someone else, and there is no one there to protect that person's reputation. God would be involved in these types of situations. This is "considering His ways." When you consider His ways, you will be better prepared to act Christ-like in a situation that God has prepared for you to become more Christ-like.

When you are reading God's Word, it is required of you to read slowly and reread what you have just read. After this, meditate on the words that you have read. Allow the Holy Spirit to reveal to you wonderful truths about life and relationships. God says that He has given you the Holy Spirit to lead and guide you into truth. You will not find God's truth through your own intellect. It must come from the Spirit.

Many Christians use the excuse that they cannot understand the Bible. Read and study the parts you do understand and other parts of the Bible will begin to be revealed to you by the Holy Spirit. For example, the birth of Christ in Luke, Chapters 1 and 2, is not that difficult, as most children know the story. But, in that story is one of the most powerful verses about God, "For no word from God will ever fail." (Luke 1:37)

c. **Delight in your decrees:** You could almost call this an oxymoron. Delight is a sign of being pleased, while decrees refer to the established laws of God. One dictionary defined decrees as "God's eternal, unchangeable, holy, wise, and sovereign purpose, comprehending at once all things that ever were or will be in their causes." I like that definition! When I read a magazine that discusses evolution, life on other planets, the vastness of millions of universes, or any other science article, it is very hard not to "delight in God's decrees." An example of this is when the article is speaking of the mathematical preciseness of the planet earth to sustain life. Another example is the theory of the God-particle that existed before the Big Bang. I don't look on these theories as man's way of explaining the laws of the universe but as God's decrees. It is astounding that there is a God who has decreed all that we sense, all that we cannot sense, and, at the same time, desires a personal relationship with each of us. Wow!

d. **Not neglect your word:** If you neglect God's word, consider the things that you would have missed. God has created a book that is like none other. No human being or group of human beings could have envisioned the contents of God's Word. This fact drives me to read and study His Word. And, the more I do, the more I find the Truth about life that I cannot find in any science or psychology book. For someone to live his or her life without God is depressing. For a Christian to live their life without reading and studying God's Word is despairing and foolish. A Christian misses the best of their life when they do not spend time in the Bible. When you see the reality and TRUTH in God's Word, you could read any atheistic book, science book, etc. and find God all over the place.

I hope you can see that God wants you to know Him as much as you can. This will require a time commitment as well as the exercise of meditation on God. I pray you will never neglect your personal reading and studying of God's Word. Your life will never be the same.

22. Where your focus should be

Since, then, you have been raised with Christ, set your hearts on things above, where Christ is, seated at the right hand of God. Set your minds on things above, not on earthly things. Colossians 3:2

These verses should be a great encouragement for you. As true Believers in Christ, the verses say that you have been raised with Christ. It is interesting that God considers you already resurrected from the dead. That is how confident

God is on your bodily resurrection. This is no small theological truth, and it is the reason that we celebrate Easter each year.

When the power of the Holy Spirit raised Jesus Christ from the dead, God was demonstrating how it will be for all Believers. You will be raised with a new body that is imperishable. I beg you to think about this truth. You will not spend eternity in a hopeless situation with constant pain and misery. You will spend eternity with God in a body that God originally intended before sin entered, and the body became diseased. Your new body will not have any diseases. This is great news for me personally. Maybe that is why I am asking you to have thoughts about your future eternity NOW! It will change your attitude.

Since you have been raised with Christ, God says to set your hearts on things above. Your "heart" is the center of emotions, dreams, desires, and wants. God says to focus on what it will be like in heaven. The only emotion that I think we will exhibit in heaven is joy that comes from praising God. There will not be anger, lust, jealousy, envy, or any other bad thought that you can have on this earth. God says to think about that joy NOW! Focus on a life that is lived full of joy. It is almost overwhelming that we human beings can experience such joy, but that is what the Bible says, because we are raised with a new body. I know many Believers worry about how you can keep from having bad thoughts in heaven – that is in the future and God will take care of you. God wants you to think on that joy-full life that you can have NOW!

These verses also say to set our minds on things above and not on the earth. This will take patience, practice, and discipline. A new habit in your life is to replace the thoughts of this world with thoughts of heaven and everything in the spiritual realm. After all, you will be spending eternity there, and God wants to get you ready for what it will be like. Our minds are our thoughts, the way we think, and what we determine is important. You are constantly choosing to think on the things that will occupy your mind. Unfortunately, the world is the greatest distracter that we have to overcome. You cannot overcome worldly thoughts with your flesh or on your own. You must start with God, Jesus Christ, and the Holy Spirit. The Spirit will bring about changes in your thinking the more that you discipline your thoughts about the spiritual realm.

If you have spare thinking time, God is saying to spend it on Him. Even when you don't have spare time, God is saying to allow the Holy Spirit to help you recognize when your thoughts are spending too much time on the things of earth. I have said this many times to many people, but reading the newspaper and listening to the news on TV is a waste of your thinking time that could be better spent on the things of God. It is for this reason that I say it must be your intentional choice to think on heaven. God will not make you think on Him. As a matter of fact, He is very disappointed in Believers who are caught up in the world and its philosophies.

All of us can make our own decision about what we allow our hearts and minds to dwell on. There is a choice. These verses are clear about what we, as Believers, need to focus on in our lives. During the day, focus your attention on who God is and what He has done for you through Jesus Christ. Think on His eternal creation. Meditate on the fact that God loves you and nothing can pluck you out of His hand. Watch your perspective change from the world (worry, anxiety, failure, negative thoughts, etc.) to His spiritual Kingdom (life, joy, peace, patience, etc.) NOW!

23. Do not trust in people – only in God

This is what the Lord says: "Cursed is the one who trusts in man, who draws strength from mere flesh and whose heart turns away from the Lord. That person will be like a bush in the wastelands; they will not see prosperity when it comes. They will dwell in the parched places of the desert, in a salt land where no one lives.

"But blessed is the one who trusts in the Lord, whose confidence is in him. They will be like a tree planted by the water that sends out its roots by the stream. It does not fear when heat comes; its leaves are always green. It has no worries in a year of drought and never fails to bear fruit." Jeremiah 17:5-8

This is a very difficult Bible passage, because it teaches something that is the exact opposite of what we learn in this world. Sometime during our life we believe that placing our trust in other people is necessary for a well-adjusted life. We trust our parents, we trust our spouse, we trust our banks, and we trust our governments (maybe I am stretching it a wee bit with the government!) When you hear God's Word says NOT to trust in any man or woman, something in you rises up and says, "No! We are suppose to trust others."

Read the Bible passage above again, and you should see why God says we cannot trust others. The theological basis for not trusting others is that everyone has sinned (draws strength from the flesh) and falls short of the glory of God (heart has turned away from God.) In other words, no matter how hard you try to live up to all of your promises to others, your dreams that you share with others, or your shared goals to reach a common objective, all of us will experience failure. Either you will fail someone or someone fails you.

If anything, to try to live up to lists of "things to do" usually results in others being disappointed in us. We can easily become disappointed in ourselves. It is for this very reason that Christ has made you free from all lists, promises, goals, etc. For example, if you are feeling the guilt or shame of letting someone else down, you cannot possibly be in God's will, because your focus is on yourself. Let it sink into your mind that you will fail others and God. God expects it and says so in His Word. He continues to love you just the way you are.

What is happening in the verses above is an encouragement for you to identify where you place your trust. Do you trust the business you work for to provide your wealth? Do you trust your spouse to always be there for you and to remain faithful? Do you trust your children not to do drugs? In all these things, God is saying to put your trust in Him. Why? He is always faithful, truthful, loving, forgiving, etc. Human beings are not.

If your trust for your happiness is placed in people and not God, you will be disappointed. This is like managing your expectations of others. You can expect people to fail you. I know this sounds negative, but it is the spiritual truth. This does not mean that you love them any less. It does not mean that you are waiting on them to fail so that you can say, "I knew it! You are a failure." NO! This is to prepare you to minister to the person who has failed. They need to know that God loves them unconditionally and you do too! The book of Hosea in the Old Testament is recommended as examples of people's failures and God's unconditional love. I would hope you take the time to read this book.

24. Know the TRUTH

Jesus answered, "I am the way, the truth, and the life. No one comes to the Father except through me." John 14:6

This is a discussion of TRUTH, because all of your philosophies about how you live your life are based on either believing what the world says or what God says. Unfortunately, most people base the way they live on the world.

The world is currently bombarded with different ways of looking at what Truth is. The Truth in this context is those foundational beliefs that a person has developed in their life that govern their behavior and influence how they make decisions. An example would be the definition of marriage. The worldview currently defines marriage as between any two adults (male and/or female). The spiritual view defines marriage as stated in the Bible—between male and female only. There are many other issues that have been defined with those two views: world or spiritual.

All Believers must reach a conviction on the spiritual view of these issues. However, many Christians will not stand on their convictions because of the possibility of being called "intolerant". When a Christian does this, I think there is severe damage to the growth of the Kingdom of God on this earth. The Kingdom of God is defined in the Bible with certain beliefs and morals. Unfortunately, we have compromised those beliefs and morals to be "politically correct." Shame on us!

In this chapter, I want to give my own overview of history that has gotten us to where we are today with worldview thinking. This overview helps me overcome most of the worldly philosophies, because I found them empty. I hope it helps you too!

Between 350BC and AD1500, the earth was considered the center of the universe. During this time, the church and state became intermingled for the sake of power of Kings ruling over the masses. The Church defined truth, and the Church said that the earth was the center of the universe and was flat. About AD1500, Copernicus discovered and proved that the earth is not the center of the universe. He used reasoning as well as research to make this claim. Naturally, the Church took an adverse position to Copernicus, because it did not want to be found wrong.

Around AD1600, Galileo confirmed the findings of Copernicus making the Church look even more foolish. About AD1700, Sir Isaac Newton put forth the idea that the universe performed like a machine. During these years, faith was being eroded by reason. Reason was becoming the tool for man to search for the meaning of his existence. God was no longer necessary to explain the universe.

By the 1800's, scientists were defining "knowledge" as only observable data; a way of thinking called "naturalism". There was little, if no, room for God, faith, miracles, etc.

In 1859, Darwin's *Origin of the Species* was published and secular humanism became a powerful method of explaining everything in the universe. Truth was only truth if it was discovered through reason and based on natural cause and effect.

However, people became disenchanted with naturalism, because it could not answer the questions concerning the life of man; for example, the purpose of man, the meaning of life, definition of values and morals, etc. There were many "soft" issues that reason and naturalism could not address: love, beauty, relationships, etc. As a result, there was the introduction of Modern Thought that presented the idea that everything is relative. Truth can only be defined by each individual in his or her own way. This sounds absolutely crazy to me, but that is what is taught in schools and colleges.

As a consequence, Absolute Truth did not exist. Truth is defined in the mind of each individual. This worldview of thinking was soon uncovered for what it was: despairing, hopeless, and empty. What has arisen is a search by individuals to try to answer the meaning of life questions. That is why there has been a recent increased interest in the "spiritual" side of living than ever before. Humanity has come to the point of knowing that there is something else out there but is still not willing to believe in God.

Today, the truth is based only on things observable; this is called science. Science deals with facts that are reliable and true. Morality and religion are based on the values that are subjective and relative to the individual. Do you see the error in this thinking? Today's world philosophy separates Knowledge from Belief. Believers should have a comprehensive worldview: God's laws cover everything in creation. Are you willing to stand on this truth as a conviction for your philosophy of life?

For the Believer, there should be no separation between the things of God and the things of this world. As a Believer, nothing lies outside the realm of God. The major challenge for Believers today is to be convicted of what they believe by FAITH. They should not try to PROVE the existence of and the work of God. HE is the WAY, TRUTH, and the LIFE. God has addressed all aspects of humanity's existence, and He has the answers for all of the questions that man can ask. It is humanity that has erroneously tried to answer those questions without the knowledge of God.

As a Christian, you have a decision to make every day as to the strength of the conviction you have concerning spiritual things. I am not asking you to be a street corner preacher (unless the Holy Spirit directs you to). I am putting forth that Christians do not need to be wimpy or shy about their spirituality. At the same time, Christians should not be judgmental about forcing their convictions on others. The Bible says that only the Holy Spirit can bring conviction to a man.

Finally, the Bible says that you shall know the Truth and the Truth shall make you free. The lie that is believed by many Christians is that this world can satisfy their needs. The truth is that only Spiritual freedom is true freedom that will allow you to live a full and abundant life.

I deeply pray that your personal convictions will become very well defined about all of the "relative" things going on in the world today. I also pray that you will become so convinced of your convictions that you will stand against all of the things that God would not be pleased with. And if anyone asks why you believe in your convictions so deeply, you will be able to explain that there are the truths you can learn from the world that are really lies, or that you can learn from the Absolute Truth provided by God.

25. Unforgiving is NOT a Christ-like attitude

For where two or three gather in my name, there am I with them." Then Peter came to Jesus and asked, "Lord, how many times shall I forgive my brother or sister who sins against me? Up to seven times?" Jesus answered, "I tell you, not seven times, but seventy-seven times. Matthew 18:20-22

People will be lovers of themselves, lovers of money, boastful, proud, abusive, disobedient to their parents, ungrateful, unholy, without love, unforgiving, slanderous, without self-control, brutal, not lovers of the good, treacherous, rash, conceited, lovers of pleasure rather than lovers of God 2 Timothy 3:2-4

"He lets her dress like a prostitute!"

"She lets him drink alcohol and stay out as late as he wants!"

"He totally ignores her and lets her play with anything."

"She buys him whatever he wants."

"I can't get him to bring her to church."

"He/She is ruining his/her life with the way he/she lives."

"I am always having to go the extra yard to buy him/her what is really needed."

"I don't know how I will ever forgive him/her for what he/she has done to me and my kids."

The above are a few comments that you have probably heard when there is a divorce. I have added children to most of the comments, because divorce has a negative impact on children.

Most of the people reading this will probably have personally experienced a divorce or have had a family member involved in a divorce. A divorce is an agreement to separate. However, the love and affection shared during the good times of a marriage usually build such a high emotional stake that separation is extremely difficult. What happens are the incidents previously described.

To protect the high emotional investment, strong feelings carry over after the divorce. It takes an extremely herculean effort to overcome these emotions and feelings that have been trampled on by another person. There is something that comes within us that says, "I've got to pay them back for what they did to me!" When this is put into the brain of a divorcee, that person CAN NEVER act in a Christ-like manner toward their ex or even other people.

This is not an evaluation of when and if Christians should divorce. I am speaking strictly about the person's attitude after divorce. It is spiritually wrong for a Christian to possess feelings of hatred, revenge, loathness, etc. toward another human being when their Savior died on the cross asking forgiveness for those who were crucifying Him. I cannot reconcile anyone's feelings toward their ex when I picture Jesus Christ forgiving the sins of both divorcees. There is no separation when Christ loves them. I do not think God accepts any excuses for not demonstrating love toward everyone especially our enemies.

The "worldly" Webster dictionary defines "unforgiving" as follows:

: not willing to forgive other people

: very harsh or difficult: not allowing weakness, error, etc.

I praise God that He does not apply that definition to me or you or anyone involved in a divorce. God forgives those that are the most difficult to forgive – YOU! Do not let your "after divorce" feelings toward your ex determine your Christ-like behavior. Let the love and peace of God flow through your entire being so that when you and your family look back at post divorce incidents, all that can be seen are the nail-scarred hands of your Lord and Savior.

26. What are you doing with your wealth?

Command those who are rich in this present world not to be arrogant nor to put their hope in wealth, which is so uncertain, but to put their hope in God, who richly provides us with everything for our enjoyment. Command them to do good, to be rich in good deeds, and to be generous and willing to share. In this way they will lay up treasure for themselves as a firm foundation for the coming age, so that they may take hold of the life that is truly life. 1 Timothy 6:17-19

The verses above speak loud and clear to those who have riches and wealth. By the way, if you live in the U.S. you are probably in the top 5% of the wealthiest people on this earth. I'm not talking about billionaires and millionaires…I'm talking about you and me…just the plain old middle class of the U.S. The first thing these verses say to us rich people is not to be arrogant about our wealth. GUILTY! GUILTY! We have all done this when we have something that someone else does not have or if we have the latest that others do not have. We become arrogant, "look what I have and you don't!" Sounds kind of childish and that is exactly what it is.

The second thing the verses say about all of us rich people is not to put our hope in our wealth. GUILTY! GUILTY! Again, we have all done this. The monthly paycheck is our only hope to keep our heads above water financially. Our 401K or retirement account is our only hope to live the kind of life in retirement that we've always wanted to live. Your paycheck and your 401k and your retirement account are all uncertain. You do not know what tomorrow may bring. The verses tell us to put our hope in God who is the real source for our enjoyment.

We can buy things that we think will bring us enjoyment. The Spiritual Truth is that God will provide the things that will bring true enjoyment. I can hear some of you saying that you have had your heart set on buying something like a boat. You could tell God that a boat would bring such enjoyment to you and your family and friends that you let ride on your boat. However, a boat brings with it additional expenses for maintenance and upkeep. You also have to park it somewhere. I guess you could claim it as a good deed when you allow inner-city children to take a ride on your boat. Only you and your heart know the truth underlying the purchase of a boat or anything that you think will bring you enjoyment. Do not forget that God said He will bring you enjoyment.

Recall the title for this chapter, "What are you doing with your wealth?" How do you spend your wealth? Is it to buy all the things that everyone else has so that you will feel important? Is it to buy something because, quite frankly, you think you deserve it! God does not get involved in becoming a CPA for your finances. He wants you to know where your wealth comes from...God! And, He wants you to be a good steward of that wealth so that He will be glorified. I think from God's perspective, wealth is measured in the value of our relationship with Him and others. Wealth is also measured in the good deeds that the wealth allows you to do. In all of these things, the use of wealth is an accurate indicator of the strength of your relationships and the number of your good deeds. Wealth, from a worldly perspective, is measured by the amount of money and things of this world that you have. Which one does your mind spend more time on—God things or worldly things? Only your heart knows the truth of your personal use of wealth.

Read the verses again. The rich, that's you and me, are commanded to do good by being rich in good deeds. These good deeds are very specific: be generous and be willing to share. By doing this, Believers will be investing in a "firm foundation for the coming age". PLUS, we will be taking hold of the life that is truly life.

27. No place for worry in a Believer's Life

"Therefore I tell you, do not worry about your life, what you will eat or drink; or about your body, what you will wear. Is not life more important than food, and the body more important than clothes? Look at the birds of the air; they do not sow or reap or store away in barns, and yet your heavenly Father feeds them. Are you not much more valuable than they? Who of you by worrying can add a single hour to his life?. . . But seek first his kingdom and his righteousness, and all these things will be given to you as well. Therefore do not worry about tomorrow, for tomorrow will worry about itself. Each day has enough trouble of its own." Matthew 6:25-34

These verses clearly put the world up against the spiritual realm and concludes that only the spiritual things should be a major part of a Christian's life.

The passage comes in the middle of what is called the "Sermon on the Mount" spoken by Jesus. There is not much more to say than what Jesus says about our priorities in living a life here on earth. He turns everything upside-down and inside out. It comes down to your perspectives of how to live life on this earth. If you, as a Christian, lived by these verses of the Bible, your life would be so different from other people. You would definitely be thought of as from another world. I do not think that would be too bad. I hope you do not either.

I have to tell you a story about my wife and me. When I get ready to go somewhere (like to church), I will walk out of the bedroom and hear my loving and beautiful wife say these words, "You're not wearing that, are you?" This is an amazing statement, because I am fully dressed and ready to go. There are some rules about matching colors and no whites before the first day of spring, and only dark colors during winter. I want to know where these rules come from. Growing up with three brothers, no one told us these rules. There are also the shirts that I finally get broken in to the point of being comfortable to wear, and she is ready to throw them in the trash. Give me a break! Maybe I'm closer to God about clothes, because I don't worry about what I am wearing.

I hope you can consider these verses when it comes to purchasing clothes and how much you spend on the brand name, rather than for the utility of what you are buying. God says He will take care of you.

All He asks and don't miss this in these verses is, "**But seek first his kingdom and his righteousness, and all these things will be given to you as well.**" There is a freedom in life that comes with thinking of God's kingdom first and not the things of this world. Remember God's Kingdom was lived vicariously through the life of Christ while He was on this earth. Therefore, I suggest you read and study the four gospels to see how Jesus lived. I do not think many of us can live the life He lived, but we sure could learn to treat other people the way He did. Just that alone would be a huge life-changing event for many of us.

The second thing not to miss is what comes immediately after this: "**Therefore do not worry about tomorrow, for tomorrow will worry about itself. Each day has enough trouble of its own.**" When I read words like these in the Bible, I am set free from this world and all of its enticements. I do not have to worry, because God has already taken care of the future.

Whenever you are worrying, it is a guarantee that your perspective is on this world and not on God. I pray that the Holy Spirit will convict you when you place more importance on the things of this world than the things of God. Put all of your faith in God and watch your life become one of peace and contentment. This is the abundant life that Jesus wants you to live.

28. Fellowship with other Believers

And let us consider how we may spur one another on toward love and good deeds, not giving up meeting together, as some are in the habit of doing, but encouraging one another—and all the more as you see the Day approaching. Hebrews 10:24-25

One of the distinguishing characteristics of Believers is that they exercise fellowship; i.e., meeting together with a purpose to encourage one another. The verse above clearly states that God encourages this activity among Believers.

An over simplification is to describe two extremes of fellowshipping. One is worldly where the goal is to eat, drink, and be merry (get drunk). At the opposite extreme is the Christian fellowship where the purpose is to grow in encouragement about living a life sold out to God. There are plenty of fellowships that fall between these two extremes but God's expectations are for Him to be recognized and honored at a fellowship with a heavy emphasis on Christians encouraging one another.

Many Christian fellowships are planned to celebrate certain holidays: Christmas, July 4, etc. May I say that a Christian fellowship does not occur without the encouragement of Christians to be strong in their faith? The beginning of the early Christian church emphasized the need for strong fellowship.

They devoted themselves to the apostles' teaching and to fellowship, to the breaking of bread and to prayer. Everyone was filled with awe at the many wonders and signs performed by the apostles. All the believers were together and had everything in common. They sold property and possessions to give to anyone who had need. Every day they continued to meet together in the temple courts. They broke bread in their homes and ate together with glad and sincere hearts, praising God and enjoying the favor of all the people. And the Lord added to their number daily those who were being saved. Acts 2:42-47

This passage is a strong support for the need for fellowship in every Believer's life. Notice that it included large groups as well smaller groups possibly consisting of two or three people. In all meetings, they ate, praised God, and encouraged one another. It even implies that other people favored their fellowships. It appears there is a belief that a Christian can go it alone in this world. Nothing could be further from the Biblical truth.

God intends that we help one another. God intends that you use your spiritual gift to help others grow in Christ. You cannot do that by keeping a distance between your brothers and sisters in Christ. You may not like to entertain – that is not the purpose of a fellowship. You may feel uncomfortable around other people – these are people who God has purposed to help you grow in Christ. Evangelism and discipleship are the two actions that Jesus assigned to the disciples (see Acts 28:18-20). These cannot be done unless there are fellowships within the Christian community. It may be that this is one reason that the church of today is not more effective. We do not take the time to encourage one another through fellowships in our homes, churches, and other places.

29. Quietness in your soul

"My heart is not proud, O Lord, my eyes are not haughty; I do not concern myself with great matters or things too wonderful for me. But I have stilled and quieted my soul; like a weaned child with its mother, like a weaned child is my soul within me. Psalm 131:1-2

These are powerful words to calm your soul. Read through them slowly. Think about your soul reaching a state of stillness and quietness. We all need this. It is something that every human being should experience. God designed us to have this need to quiet our soul. Otherwise, pride and arrogance will live continually in our soul negatively impacting our relationship with others. The verses above will, hopefully, bring a soothing effect to your soul.

Your soul can rest secure, like a child with its mother, when you and God are one within your soul. Pay attention to the needs of your soul. Your soul is who you are to others. You can call it your personality that consists of your emotions and thoughts. Also, our decisions communicate to others who we are and how we are feeling. I can think of a child who is worrying their mother to the point that the mother cannot show the love and care for that child ,because her own soul is disquieted. The mother is almost like a different person, because she is allowing a temporary situation to dictate the condition of her soul.

Our lives can be filled with busyness and activities. One thing that we all should consider is the real human need for quietness of our soul. Do not become enslaved to thoughts of what we have accomplished or what we possess. Let us not become dictated to by schedules of "great matters". Rather, still yourself so that God can comfort you and give you peace that is beyond this world.

God intended for us to humble ourselves with others, so that there is a peace that passes all understanding. There are other people who have gone through what you are going through or even worse things. We do not need to be so proud or haughty that we hide our true feelings. This is especially true to those who we love and are near to us. Why is it that we cannot be open and honest with others? Especially, with those who are dear to us?

There is also our need to depend upon God who has given us blessings and riches beyond our imagination. We can call upon God when we are at our lowest to bring people into our lives that we need for those special moments. God will provide for you. He does not like to see any of His children disquieted in their soul. At the same time, others need the stillness and quietness of your soul to see that there is hope in this world, the hope that comes from God through Jesus Christ who is in you.

As a disciple of Christ, be at peace at all times by trusting God completely. Others will see Jesus in your soul and will want that same quietness for their soul. The song, "Silent Night" is all about quieting the soul: calmness and peace. You may want to consider this song as an all year song and not just at Christmas. I pray you experience the Holy Spirit quietness in your soul that God gives us through His Son, Jesus Christ.

30. Practical living in today's world

Keep reminding God's people of these things. Warn them before God against quarreling about words; it is of no value, and only ruins those who listen. Do your best to present yourself to God as one approved, a worker who does not need to be ashamed and who correctly handles the word of truth. Avoid godless chatter, because those who indulge in it will become more and more ungodly. Their teaching will spread like gangrene. Among them are Hymenaeus and Philetus, who have departed from the truth. They say that the resurrection has already taken place, and they destroy the faith of some. " 2 Timothy 2:14-18

The content of the Bible passage above is very practical. The Bible passage applies to all of our lives if we will stop and take a moment to focus on some key words: keep reminding; warn; quarreling; a worker approved; not ashamed; correctly handles the word of truth; avoid godless chatter; departed from the truth; and, destroy the faith of another. You could have picked different words or phrases, but I believe these nine words/phrases provide a reasonable description of a modern day Christian like you or me.

"Keep reminding," sounds like something you would say to describe working with children. Parents, teachers, coaches, and any others working with kids do this at least ten times per day. Obviously, children forget or things just don't register with them. We have to keep reminding them to brush their teeth, clean their room, make their bed, etc. In the context above, we are to keep reminding ADULT Christians! No one is exempt from being reminded about certain things in their Christian life. In this chapter, I will be reminding you of at least nine practical aspects of your Christian life.

One thing that has helped me is to be involved in a "mentoring" relationship with another man. I have been involved in mentoring men for 35 years, and I have no idea how any man or woman can be a strong Christian without having someone to remind her/him of certain things. If you think about it, many people suggest ways to remember something by putting a note on the mirror in the bathroom or on the refrigerator. Let us all agree that we need someone to "keep reminding" us of Christian living. A mirror or a refrigerator or any other inanimate object will never replace a real live person. By meeting with another person on a regular basis, both of you will get to know the other to the point of being candid and factual about your spiritual life. When you finally understand that God says to "keep reminding", I hope you do not mind if I add, "keep mentoring".

What are you to be reminded of or what are you to remind someone else of? Warn other Christians regarding quarreling over words. Do not be argumentative. Relationships with others are at the heart of this warning. God asks you to have a strong healthy relationship with everyone. I know you are thinking of some relative or neighbor that is impossible to relate to, but God does not exclude anyone from your life. You are here for the purpose of being used by God. You must not quarrel because it ruins relationships. Consider yourself warned by me.

The next set of words and phrases encourage you to work diligently with integrity and honesty. Do nothing at work that would cause you shame. For example, don't take pens and pencils home to be used by your children for school. Do not play computer games during company time. Paul's letter was written to encourage Timothy as a Pastor in his ministry for God. Since we all have a spiritual gift, we all have a ministry also. When it says to correctly handle the word of truth, it is speaking of the Bible. Basically, there is no way any Believer can escape the need to read and study the Word of God. It must be a necessary part of your life.

If there is one thing that goes on whenever two or more are gathered in this world, it is discussions of the latest news and sports. Remember, no quarreling words over whose team is better! God says that the only thing that godless chatter will get you is that you will become more ungodly. I hope you can see the truth of this in your own life. Please do not judge someone else as these words are addressed to you and me. It is also not uncommon for religion to become a hot topic for discussion. However, there have been so many "lines drawn in the sand" over religious issues, it is difficult to know what to believe. It is easy to become persuaded by something that sounds like the truth but it is not.

One example is the idea that there are many "personal" ways to go to heaven. Jesus is only one way. This truth comes from giving the self the latitude to decide what is truth. Your "self" replaces God's Word and God Himself. Actually, your "self" replaces anything that doesn't fit what you think is truth. You can become easy prey when the adversary appeals to your flesh. The reason this is so dangerous to every Christian is that you can lead others astray. This is one reason we have so many different kinds of churches, denominations, and cults. Please be on guard and know the Word of God.

I hope this chapter has helped you realize the importance of sharing with other Christians. I do not think that most Believers realize how practical God is when it comes to living a Christian life on this earth. In summary, God hates quarreling, but He loves relationships. God hates dishonesty, but He loves the respected person at work. God hates the untruths that sway true Believers, but He loves those who read and study His Word. I hope these are practical descriptions of your Christian life. If they are not, I pray that you will make some life-changing decisions to make your relationship with God strong and healthy.

31. God intentionally tests your faith through suffering

In all this you greatly rejoice, though now for a little while you may have had to suffer grief in all kinds of trials. These have come so that the proven genuineness of your faith—of greater worth than gold, which perishes even though refined by fire—may result in praise, glory and honor when Jesus Christ is revealed. 1 Peter 1:6-7

Do you see two great spiritual truths in these Bible verses?

1. You will have to suffer grief in all kinds of trials.

2. When you are suffering, you are to greatly rejoice.

These two spiritual truths beg the question, "How can I rejoice greatly when suffering?" Jesus rejoiced greatly at the death of Lazarus because His father was to be glorified after the resurrection of Lazarus. The angels rejoiced at the birth of Christ although His life would lead to the cross. As human beings, we have limited insight into the spiritual things that impact us. Maybe this is why spiritual growth seems so slow and difficult?

God's spiritual insight is complete and without error. He sees the future end product of His children who are mature in the faith and can actually encourage others during the most difficult of times. Personally, I know that God has provided encouragement to me through the growth in faith that occurred while others were growing through suffering. At the same time, I have been told about my encouragement to others with my personal suffering. What is interesting about this encouragement is that it must come from the Holy Spirit, because I am praying and suffering during my own suffering. Even Jesus knew that He must suffer so that we might be encouraged through His suffering. If you can see this, then you are probably experiencing the word "encouragement", and your faith is being tested to strengthen it.

There are more spiritual truths in these two Bible verses:

1. Your faith is much more valuable than gold

2. Sufferings purify and strengthens your faith

As Believers, we do not meditate on the truth that things of the Spirit are more valuable than three-dimensional worldly objects. God is amazing in declaring this truth in His sovereignty. All Believers should be asking the Holy Spirit to reveal that things of this world have less value than the things of the Spirit. We cannot have fellowship with God without living out this truth in our daily lives. At the same time, God has made it clear that our faith should increase in purity. This truly excites me that God has made this possible. My faith comes from God through tests and sufferings. My faith continues to be strengthened as I realize that the suffering is intended to encourage others. Faith without any impurities is the goal that God has set for each of us. He allows sufferings to remove the impurities of my faith. With the world so unbelievably contaminated, I yearn for the purity of my faith.

The final spiritual truth is that your genuine faith results in praise, honor, and glory for Jesus. Whenever I make that statement, I believe that it is the ultimate in moving closer to God. Without removing our faith impurities, I do not see how we can grow closer to God. I want to be near God, and I hope you do too! Therefore, accept the sufferings so that your faith continues to be refined and become purer and purer.

SECTION 4

The Spiritual Concept Of Death

Introduction

The reality of death is one of the most feared life-style changes that humanity has to come to grips with. Many people worry about their own death. They become engrossed in how they might die and/or how they might have to live before they die. Others are trying to learn to cope with the death of a loved one. This could be a parent, a spouse, or, one of the most devastating, the death of a child. Since death has such a strangle hold on humanity, I wanted to devote an entire section to the concept of death, especially, from a spiritual point of view.

When Jesus was resurrected, He changed forever how Christians should view death. The most astounding statements in the Bible about resurrection come from 1 Corinthians 15. This particular chapter should be a monthly read for all Christians. The Bible says that Believers will be resurrected to a new life with a body like Jesus. This is difficult to comprehend since our bodies grow older and weaker with age. A new resurrected body like Christ is a promise from God. Using 1 Corinthians 15 and other scripture, I want to discuss the following aspects of death:

- Death is not a "downer" for Christians, but is a time of celebration
- A Believer will live eternally with God
- How to grow old gracefully

- The End Times as defined by God are getting closer
- Your current body will return to dust, but will be raised as a super body
- How does God view suicide and cremation?
- Unbelievers will face a final judgment without a second chance, but will experience a Second Death – eternal separation from God
- Believers will be judged and rewarded for their acts as a Christian while living on this earth
- Believers will receive crowns for their acts of righteousness

My intent is that these discussions will give you a strong spiritual understanding of death as presented in the Bible. My prayer is that your mind will be renewed to live your life on this earth to life's fullest because: "Where, O death, is your victory? Were, O death, is your sting?" (1 Corinthians 15:55)

1. Life and Death: The Greatest and the Worst

Jesus said to her, "I am the resurrection and the life. The one who believes in me will live, even though they die; and whoever lives by believing in me will never die. Do you believe this?" John 11:25-26

This is a favorite story from the New Testament. It concerns the death of one of Jesus' closest friends, Lazarus. His two sisters had sent for Jesus to heal Lazarus before he died. Jesus delayed His coming and Lazarus died. [Note: God has a purpose in everything, even in death.] Jesus answered Mary and Martha with words that all of us Believers should ponder in our minds when we experience the death of a close loved one.

Jesus was talking to Martha about Him being the resurrection. He told her that he was the resurrection and the life, and that through belief in him no one would truly die. Read this last sentence again and again..."through belief in Jesus no one would truly die." These are extremely comforting words for Martha and Mary and for you and me today.

Most people would agree with the title of this chapter as, "Life and Death: The Greatest and the Worst." However, for Believers, we would have to disagree. Life is the Greatest but death is the Greatest of the Greatest. By the time you have finished reading this, I hope your spiritual perspective of this statement is in agreement with the Bible passage above. It will be very difficult for you to accept this, but not impossible. Especially, if you have lost a very close loved one on or near a Holiday with Christmas or their birthday being the most emotionally significant.

The beginning of life is one of the most joyous, awe-inspiring events in everyone's life. There is nothing sweeter than to hold a newborn baby. I am a grandfather with experience in this matter, and there is nothing like it. God has provided life to a human being and many people, as well as all of the angels in heaven, are singing and celebrating this new life. Therefore, I, and most of you would agree that "life" is the Greatest. I think we would be wrong. Read on...

If we move along in time with that baby growing into a child, an adolescent, and, finally, an adult, we will find lots of ups and downs as far as life goes. The world offers nothing but hard work and stressful times due to our dependence on having enough money just to live on from day to day. As Believers, God says that He desires our lives here on earth to be "abundant and full". This requires a total dependence on God and not this world. This spiritual truth is a hard lesson to learn for most adult Believers. Children have no problem with it...they trust God implicitly. Unfortunately, we Adults become more "selfish" oriented and begin to expect good things to happen to us. Some of us actually get to the point of challenging and defying God when death of a loved one occurs. This brings me to the second part of the above title.

As brutally honest as I can be, death to any Believer should not be a "downer." It is the Greatest of the Greatest events in a Believer's life. Any Believer who dies before we do goes immediately into the presence of God. I do not know how that makes you feel, but anything less than a celebration is not recognizing the greatly improved life of the one who died. If you have a problem with this statement, then I suggest you spend more time thinking of heaven and not earth. The one who has died can see us and would love to tell us how great everything is. There is a purpose that God had for creating everything – He wants a strong, loving, intimate, and growing relationship with each one of us. That relationship becomes an ultimate reality when you die. Paul did not really want to wait on God's timing for his death. He wanted to go to heaven as soon as possible to remove himself from this sin-infested cesspool called the world.

For some reason or other, many Believers believe the lie of Satan that, on this world, it "doesn't get any better than this." What a rotten, low-down, stinking lie. What is worse is that we will base the way we live on that lie. One of the most deceitful lies that Satan will tell a person who has lost a close loved one is "look at what you are going to miss about that person." Do not misunderstand what I am trying to say. Remembering a lost loved one is one of God's ways of ministering to you. He wants you to remember that person and all of the good times spent together. But, I think this "remembrance" is to increase your thoughts of heaven and the reunion that will occur when you die. It is not to look at the things that had yet to happen to that person and you missed them. You think more of yourself (selfishness) instead of your loved one who is seeing Jesus Christ every eternal day of their life.

Satan would rather have you think of all the things that you will miss about that person. Missing someone is absolutely acceptable to the point that you long to be with him or her in heaven...not in this world. Let me say this again, the world is not my choice for where I would like to spend eternity with my family. People who go on to heaven before us would love to tell us that. God has provided these words in the Bible. The way we live our lives on earth after the death of a loved one should be based on longing to be with them in heaven. This produces a greater personal testimony about your loved one.

God has purposed for you to remain on earth to continue to be a witness for Him. You have a Godly purpose that is stronger than any purpose you have had in your life. You can testify to others who need to hear that God took your loved one according to His Plan for Eternity. I cannot tell you what an awesome responsibility you have to testify about when you die, there will be angels singing in heaven and, hopefully, your loved ones on earth will be celebrating your new eternal life with Christ. I am getting so excited about seeing my loved ones in heaven that if I keep writing, I am tempted to ask God to go ahead and take me. But, He has work for me to do; so, in this world I must remain.

Personal testimony: my grandfather, who I loved greatly, was born on Christmas day. I was 12 when he died, and I remember crying like a baby. I was thinking only of how I would miss him. I did not think of him in heaven. My mother died when I was 20 years old. I barely cried at her funeral. Quite frankly, I knew my grandfather better than my own mother. This was because she took care of me, and I grew very desensitized to her relationship with me. Today, I miss many things about our relationship. Four years before she died, I was away from home going to college. I did not get to know her as an adult. To me, she was my caretaker. I wish I had more talks with her. She died on May 16 and frequently Mothers' Day is celebrated on the day she died. It is very hard to avoid the thoughts and emotions that go through my mind. As I have matured as a Christian, my longing to see her in heaven is beyond words. My thoughts have gone from what I missed (bordering on selfishness) to full of hope when I will see her again in heaven. I can hardly wait! Therefore, my reason for living today is to give God all the glory for the thing called "death." Jesus Christ was resurrected and has conquered death for all Believers.

"Where, O death, is your victory? Where, O death, is your sting?"

Praise the Lord and celebrate the loss of a close loved one. God is always at work, and He has everything taken care of, including the rest of your life. Think of your loved one who has died as God's way of telling you that there is a heaven, and He wants you to be hard at work in spreading the Kingdom of God on this earth until He takes you to heaven through a doorway called death.

2. Spiritual maturity is God's remedy for growing old

Therefore we do not lose heart. Though outwardly we are wasting away, yet inwardly we are being renewed day by day. For our light and momentary troubles are achieving for us an eternal glory that far outweighs them all. So we fix our eyes not on what is seen, but on what is unseen, since what is seen is temporary, but what is unseen is eternal. 2 Corinthians 4:16-18

These are very interesting verses that talk about how our bodies waste away as we grow older. They also address the troubles we have while we live on this earth. Finally, they tell us what God has given us as a remedy for the associated mental despair and depression that can occur as we grow older and cannot do the things that we were able to do when we were younger. This one hits way too close to home...me! I think that someone should write a book that lists what a 68-year-old man should not be doing that he used to do (e.g., climbing ladders, swinging axes, etc.)

Before anyone thinks they are too young to read this write-up, there are things that an 18 year old cannot do that they could do when they were 10. An example is simple constant motion with no regard to sleep. It is hard to get a 10 year old to go to sleep no matter how tired they are, and it is just as hard to get an 18 year old out of bed in the morning, because they feel so tired. Something has aged that person and physical decline will continue to occur until they die.

The Bible says that everyone will die. Even science agrees with the Bible that everyone will die. We will all die someday. If I keep saying the word "die", you will probably start to get depressed. Christians do not need to get depressed or feel hopeless or live in despair about the future involving physical death. Thankfully, God has made it possible for us to die. When Adam and Eve sinned, God did not want them to live forever with their fear and guilt of sin. To remedy this, He removed them from the Garden of Eden that contained the Tree of Life. Man can now die without living forever in a sinful state on this earth. We should all thank God for physical death.

In the verse above, God says not to lose heart. Growing old can be a real downer to a person who values the way they look and the things they can do. Women are extremely concerned about looking young. Wrinkles, extra weight, and hair color changes can be devastating to a woman's self-esteem. For men, it is usually the mid section that seems to expand and their physical prowess is degraded. But God says not to lose heart, because He wants you fix your eyes on the spiritual realm and not the physical realm.

As we age, our Christian principles should be more clearly defined, and our conviction to those principles should be stronger. This is why young people usually consider older people as inflexible when it is really a strengthening of convictions. I would call this being renewed day by day as the verses above state. God wants to remove the world from us as Christians and replace it with Christ-like qualities. This is aging. I like it that God says "daily". This means that He is always working on me and renewing me every day of my Christian life. He is getting you and me ready for heaven where there will no longer be sin and death.

The verses above also talk about the troubles we have in this world. I personally have several minor physical issues that will probably be with me the rest of my life. There have also been times of severe pain and serious illnesses. God says to consider (think hard about) all of these troubles as momentary and light.

One thing that I have not done very well when I am physically hurting is to get my mind off myself and put it on God and others. I have learned that when I talk a lot about my troubles, they seem to get worse. When I focus on God or others, the troubles are almost forgotten. The less I can talk about my troubles, the more I can focus on the spiritual realm. Also, I need to think more about the eternal glory awaiting me in heaven rather than my troubles here on this earth.

Finally, God says to fix our eyes on what is unseen (the spiritual realm) instead of what is seen (everything in this physical world). This is God's remedy for aging: start thinking about eternity and heaven now regardless of your current age. I think most Christians say that they will wait until they retire, and then start thinking about those things. This is most unfortunate, because the impact of aging may be stronger than your ability to fix your eyes on the unseen.

I think God is saying to every Christian to get your mind off the world and put it in heaven. I think He is saying to live your heavenly life right now while you are living on this earth. By doing this, you will not suffer from the negative side effects of aging and the devastation of physical problems. Begin as soon as you can to put things in your life that will remind you of the unseen: God, Jesus Christ, the Holy Spirit, eternal life, heaven, eternity, etc. The sooner you do this in your life, the more abundant your life will be on this earth. This all makes a lot of sense to me as a spiritual truth that every Christian must learn. I pray you will live in eternity while you are living now.

3. Your current body will return to dust

Then the Lord God formed a man from the dust of the ground and breathed into his nostrils the breath of life, and the man became a living being. Genesis 2:7

God says that He created you from dust and to dust you will return. Millions of people have studied the physical body, and billions of dollars have been spent to find solutions to the diseases of the body. As soon as the body is born, it begins to die. Some humans are preoccupied with the desire to keep their bodies young in appearance, but their body will still die. Many people spend huge amounts of money to try to live longer or look younger. However, the Bible and the most atheistic person in the world are in agreement that the physical body will die and return to dust.

God declared that our bodies would die because of sin. He did not want us to live with the guilt and shame of sin for an eternity. God told Adam **"but you must not eat from the tree of the knowledge of good and evil, for when you**

eat from it you will certainly die." (Genesis 2:17) Please understand that the spiritual meaning of "death" or "to die" is to "become separated." When you die physically, you are separated from this world and your loved ones. In addition, the Bible uses a word meaning "to sleep" for Believers who die. Death is not a final word on your life.

God's purpose for our bodies is to be able to interact with the physical world. The five basic senses of our body are windows as to how we interact with the world. What is fascinating, from God's creation of humans, is that our physical bodies reveal the condition of our souls to other people. This is a major aspect of how we live our lives and interact with others. Other people see anger, depression, joy, humility, and all other soul characteristics through our physical bodies. Non-verbal behavior represents a huge percentage of how we communicate. We can try to hide our feelings, but all of us will become exhausted in putting up a false front.

The Bible is clear that your earthly body is temporary. It is referred to as a tent that is considered a temporary structure. **"I think it is right to refresh your memory as long as I live in the tent of this body, because I know that I will soon put it aside, as our Lord Jesus Christ has made clear to me."** 2 Peter 1:13-14

This temporary body that we now have is to be the dwelling place for your soul and your spirit on this earth. In the case of a Believer, the body will be the dwelling place for the Holy Spirit. This is a strong point emphasized by Jesus Christ. The Believer's body is also referred to as the temple of the Holy Spirit. **"Do you not know that your bodies are temples of the Holy Spirit, who is in you, whom you have received from God?"** 1 Corinthians 6:19-20

The body contains some of the natural drives that God has given us. The motive for sexual activity is a major part of God's command to replenish the earth. However, we all know that this God-ordained desire has been abused and misused by humanity resulting in all manners of sin. Since this body will die, God has declared that one day He will resurrect our physical bodies. Surprisingly, He will do this for both Believers and unbelievers.

Many Believers have a tough time handling the topic of cremation. After reading this chapter on our bodies returning to dust, it should be obvious that ashes from cremation are not that different than dust on the ground. No matter what happens to a believer's body after death, I have a firm belief that God can speak all of the molecules and cells of our bodies back into existence. This would be the same miracle as when He created us at the beginning of our lives. Cremation is a personal decision that God can manage no matter what a person does with their body.

4. Your resurrected body will be like "Superman"

For we know that if the earthly tent we live in is destroyed, we have a building from God, an eternal house in heaven, not built by human hands. 2 Corinthians 5:1

The concept of our resurrected bodies is strange and wonderful. Many Believers have a difficult time accepting the Biblical fact that God will change their earthly body into a glorified body that will be just like the glorified body of Christ. For this reason, I am including an abundance of Bible verses that support the idea of your glorified body. A fundamental fact about needing a glorified body is to remove the temptations that our earthly body continued to unmercifully pound at us while we were living on earth.

When we live in the Presence of God, there can be no sin and, therefore, no temptations originating from a worldly body. God will remove Satan as a tempter for eternity. The only other thing that is needed to live with Him for an eternity is to change the body into a glorified body. A quick Biblical reference for the resurrected body is 1 Corinthians, Chapter 15. I recommend you read that chapter frequently and soak in the miraculous work that God will do with your body.

So will it be with the resurrection of the dead. The body that is sown is perishable, it is raised imperishable; it is sown in dishonor, it is raised in glory; it is sown in weakness, it is raised in power; it is sown a natural body, it is raised a spiritual body. If there is a natural body, there is also a spiritual body. 1 Corinthians 15:42-44

Read these words about your future body. It will be imperishable; i.e., it will be immortal and will not suffer death. It will be raised in glory; i.e., the removal of the stain and guilt of sin. It will shine as a star in the sky. It will be raised in power. Men must love to hear this. There will be incomparable strength with the body and no weakness. Finally it will be a spiritual body. This is required since

God is a Spirit; we must have a spiritual body. However (and a strong "however"), our souls will continue to be unique to who we are.

And just as we have borne the image of the earthly man, so shall we bear the image of the heavenly man. 1 Corinthians 15:42-49

This is an amazing statement that I have a difficult time accepting. Our bodies will be "the image of the heavenly man". Who is that man? Jesus Christ. This is a tremendous gift from God to His creation, man. It is too much to comprehend in our current worldly bodies, but one day all Believers will have a glorified body created by God. Praise the Lord!

5. Death in the life of a Believer and an unbeliever

Listen, I tell you a mystery: We will not all sleep, but we will all be changed—in a flash, in the twinkling of an eye, at the last trumpet. For the trumpet will sound, the dead will be raised imperishable, and we will be changed. For the perishable must clothe itself with the imperishable, and the mortal with immortality. 1 Corinthians 15:51-53

This continues the Biblical support for the amazing, mysterious, unbelievable, wonderful glorified body that God has planned for every Believer. However, it surprises me that God will also resurrect the bodies of unbelievers for judgment.

Then I saw a great white throne and him who was seated on it. And I saw the dead, great and small, standing before the throne, and books were opened. Another book was opened, which is the book of life. The dead were judged according to what they had done as recorded in the books. The sea gave up the dead that were in it, and death and Hades gave up the dead that were in them, and each person was judged according to what they had done. Then death and Hades were thrown into the lake of fire. The lake of fire is the second death. Anyone whose name was not found written in the book of life was thrown into the lake of fire. Revelation 20:11-15

When God is prepared to judge mankind, all bodies are resurrected. No matter how many times a human body decomposes in the sea, God will resurrect that body. Believers will not be a part of this judgment, because the blood of Christ has atoned for their sins. Their sins against God were forgiven when Christ died on the cross and presented His blood on the perfect altar made without human hands in heaven. (See Hebrews 8-10) God will allow every unbeliever to present reasons for why they should live eternally with God. However, if their name does not appear in the Book of Life, then that person will face the Second Death. This judgment of unbelievers is not a Second Chance but is the Second Death. Remember that "death" in the Bible means separation. In this case, the unbeliever is removed from the Presence of God for eternity and thrown into the Lake of fire with Satan and all other evil forces.

I want to end this discussion of the human body with additional scripture that speaks of the immortality for the Believer. **When the perishable has been clothed with the imperishable, and the mortal with immortality, then the saying that is written will come true: "Death has been swallowed up in victory." "Where, O death, is your victory? Where, O death, is your sting?" The sting of death is sin, and the power of sin is the law. But thanks be to God! He gives us the victory through our Lord Jesus Christ.** 1 Corinthians 15:54-56 Death has no hold on Believers, and they will not suffer the Second Death. Only unbelievers will face the Second Death.

AMEN! and AMEN! All glory to God! He has a wonderful plan for your body.

6. God has forgiven people who commit suicide

Let me state up front that God's forgiveness of sins includes the sin of suicide. I will support this position with Biblical passages and examples. You may disagree with my position on suicide. All I ask is that you support your conclusions with Biblical passages.

God hates sin. Suicide is a sin. Therefore, God hates suicide. Suicide is never the answer to life's problems. Anyone considering suicide should always seek professional counseling. There are too many people who are left behind that have to assess the "why" a person thought suicide was the answer to all of their problems. It is one of the most selfish actions that a person can take, and it is always an unexplainable death.

People develop explanations for suicide, not for truth, but for shelter or self-protection; i.e., to try to feel comfortable about the actions of another person. In doing this, they build a house of cards, rather than find refuge in an unshakable shelter...the love of God. You can find refuge in a safe place of unfailing love. I want to direct you to the One, Jesus Christ, whose compassion for each of us is an unmovable peace.

Though a feeling of despair is not uncommon, it is a sin to take a life. All life is sacred. God creates all life. All human life is created in the image of God. You and I are so special to God that He gave His only Son to die on a cross so that we might be forgiven of our sins. What I am saying are some tough words but all are truths from God's Word.

Genesis 1:26, **"Then God said, "Let us make man in our own image, in our likeness."**

Exodus 20:23, **"you shall not murder."**

Romans 20:13, **"everything that does not come from faith is sin."**

In the Sermon on the Mount (Matthew, chapters 5-7), Jesus defined murder to include being angry with someone. With that in mind, I would not doubt that every Believer has committed murder. To take one's own life, because we have come to the end of our resources is to deny the resources of God. It is a faltering in our faith. Tradition has defined suicide as the unpardonable sin using what Jesus said in Mark 3:28-29:

"Truly I tell you, people can be forgiven all their sins and every slander they utter, but whoever blasphemes against the Holy Spirit will never be forgiven; they are guilty of an eternal sin."

The key words in this passage are, "blasphemes against the Holy Spirit." This is the one sin that will not be forgiven. The word "blasphemes" means to reject the work of the Holy Spirit. What is the work of the Holy Spirit?

"When the Advocate [Holy Spirit] comes, whom I will send to you from the Father—the Spirit of truth who goes out from the Father—he will testify about me. John 15:26

Blaspheming the Holy Spirit is to reject Jesus Christ and His testimony. It is to reject the only way to God and heaven. God cannot forgive someone who rejects the message of the gospel.

No single sin, not even the taking of a life (murder), evicts a person from heaven into hell. What sort of momentary weakness, what brief cloud of hopelessness can cause a person to take his or her own life will always be a mystery. But no one can say this: that the person's final act is unforgivable. All sins will be forgiven if they give up resisting the Spirit and look to Jesus for salvation.

7. After death, there is no second chance

I, even I, am he who blots our your transgressions, for my own sake, and remembers your sins no more. Review the past for me, let us argue the matter together; state the case for your innocence. Isaiah 43:25

Then I saw a great white throne and him who was seated on it. The earth and the heavens fled from his presence, and there was no place for them. And I saw the dead, great and small, standing before the throne, and books were opened. Another book was opened, which is the book of life. The dead were judged according to what they had done as recorded in the books. The sea gave up the dead that were in it, and death and Hades gave up the dead that were in them, and each person was judged according to what they had done. Then death and Hades were thrown into the lake of fire. The lake of fire is the second death. Anyone whose name was not found written in the book of life was thrown into the lake of fire. Revelation 20:11-15

These are very sobering words from God. During the Old Testament and until Jesus died on the cross in the New Testament, Believers could not go to heaven when they physically died. They were sinners, and their sins had not been reconciled to God. God saw them as sinners needing a Savior. As long as their sins were present, they could not be with God in heaven. Christ had not paid for their sins.

This is why God told Abraham that Abraham's faith was "credited" it to him as righteousness (Genesis 15:6). What happened to Believers who died before Christ paid for their sins? The answer can be clearly found in the words of Christ Himself. Please stop and read what Jesus says in Luke 16:19-30. The following is an explanation of that Bible passage. The place that all dead people went was called Hades or Sheol. Sheol or Hades is referenced as the place of the dead (both Believes and non-Believers). When you read Luke 16:19-30, Jesus says that Lazarus was in Abraham's bosom while the rich man was in the "Place of Torment". You can picture this as two compartments with a huge impassable ditch between the two compartments. Abraham's bosom could also be Paradise referenced by Jesus on the cross to the thief; see Luke 23:43. Or, Paradise could be heaven. In either place, you will be with Jesus.

The Old Testament Believers were kept on the "Abraham's Bosom" side. After Christ died on the cross, Jesus went to Heaven with His blood. (See Hebrews, Chapter 9) The moment He put His precious, pure, and innocent blood on the Heavenly Altar not made with human hands, ALL sins for ALL human beings were forgiven. This is the good news for all human beings! Glory Hallelujah! Praise the Lord! His blood covered over all of your sins and my sins (past, present, and all those in the future.)

God has restored His relationship with us through the blood of Christ on that Heavenly altar (see Hebrews, Chapters 8-10). All Believers were now ready to go to heaven to be with God. Their sins had been paid for and they could stand sinless before a holy God. Sometime after Jesus was crucified and before His resurrection, Jesus went to Abraham's Bosom, and brought all of the Believers who had believed on "credit" to heaven. With the "credit" paid in full, Jesus was able to go to Hades and bring all of the Old Testament saints to heaven; remember the thief on the cross (read Ephesians 4:7-10.)

All New Testament Christians will go directly to heaven when they die. Abraham's Bosom in Hades is empty! However, the "Place of Torment" continues to be filled with millions of people because of their rejection of God and His revelations. These people are not in "hell" yet. The "Place of Torment" is not hell. Hell is the "lake of fire" as described in the verses from the book of Revelation (see Revelation 20:11-15). In this reference, it says that "Hades gave up the dead" and everyone was judged. They were judged based on their works. After each person was judged, they were thrown into the "lake of fire"–eternal separation from God. Also, note that Hades was also thrown into the "lake of fire.

There is no second chance for someone standing before God and giving an accounting of their works while they lived on earth. For every good work, God will show them a time when they rejected His revelation of who He is. Although NOT in the Bible, I believe that God will allow a person to stand there for 1,000 years or longer trying to convince God that he/she is worthy of being in heaven... not a chance! Only their believing about that drop of blood on the Heavenly Altar could give them access to an eternity with God.

The Bible says that at the name of Jesus, every knee shall bow. Although not specifically in the Bible, I believe that the person standing before God at this Final Judgment will reach a point of finally understanding who God is and what Jesus Christ did for them. At that moment, they will bow their knees to our Lord and Savior Jesus Christ. But, it's too late. Part of the eternal torment that they will feel in the Lake of Fire will be their own stubbornness, pride, and self-effacing way of life that they lived on earth and not living the life of a Believer. They will know it, see it clearly, and live with it every day in eternity. What a thought for eternal torment!

How about you? Do you identify with the Believers who will spend eternity in Heaven with God, or are you getting your list of works ready to argue with God on why you should be in heaven? For Believers, it is imperative that we share these truths with others. They will have to decide for themselves for God will hold everyone personally accountable for the way they lived their life on this earth: a self-denial life lived for Christ, or a selfish life lived for themselves. These are very sobering words.

8. Rewards on earth or rewards from the Lord?

Therefore we are always confident and know that as long as we are at home in the body we are away from the Lord. For we live by faith, not by sight. We are confident, I say, and would prefer to be away from the body and at home with the Lord. So we make it our goal to please him, whether we are at home in the body or away from it. For we must all appear before the judgment seat of Christ, so that each of us may receive what is due us for the things done while in the body, whether good or bad. 2 Corinthians 5:6-10

There are numerous spiritual truths in this Bible passage, and I will discuss each one of them. However, my main objective is that Christ will judge Christians in all that they do after becoming a Christian. I will get to this objective later, but let me explain some of the other verses.

According to the verses above, a Christian can be in only one of two places: either in their physical body here on earth or living with Christ in heaven. There is no other place to find a Christian. Paul wrote these thoughts with confidence. He was convinced that if he was in his physical body then he could not be with the Lord. He went so far as to say that Christians should prefer to be away from their physical body (dead) and to be with Christ.

This is a difficult thought for many Christians. We become so enamored and influenced by the world that we do not even think about being with Christ in heaven. Christians have a different perspective of their death. Paul is basically saying that physical death is nothing to a Christian from an earthly point of view, but death is fantastic from a heavenly perspective. It is this kind of thinking that Paul has to add that Christians must live by faith and not by sight. In other words, we live each day knowing that if our heart stopped beating, we would immediately be in the presence of Christ. This is an infinitely better place to be than on this earth. I am disappointed that many Christians have not digested this spiritual truth and made it part of their lives. This is a magnificent promise from God.

As long as we are living and breathing on this earth, God has expectations of what we should be doing as Believers. In everything, we should be trying to please Him. This is an important goal for every Christian, because each of us will face the judgment seat of Christ. Do not confuse this judgment with the judgment of your sins. The judgment for sins occurs at the Great White Throne judgment that is described in Revelation 20. As a Christian, Christ forgave your sins through His taking on the judgment meant for you for your sins. You will not be judged for your sins. They do not exist with God because of the work of Christ on the cross. As a Christian you will not be a participant in the Great White Throne judgment.

However, you (and every other Christian) will be judged for the works that you do as a Christian. I think this is a little known and little understood spiritual truth about our being Christians on this earth. Everything we do while we are still in our physical bodies will be part of a future judgment by Christ. Jesus referred to this spiritual truth as follows:

> **Be careful not to practice your righteousness in front of others to be seen by them. If you do, you will have no reward from your Father in heaven. "So when you give to the needy, do not announce it with trumpets, as the hypocrites do in**

the synagogues and on the streets, to be honored by others. Truly I tell you, they have received their reward in full. But when you give to the needy, do not let your left hand know what your right hand is doing, so that your giving may be in secret. Then your Father, who sees what is done in secret, will reward you. Matthew 6:1-4

Jesus is saying that if you receive a reward for doing good works on earth, then you have received your reward. Everything you do without recognition on earth will be considered as worthy of a reward that God will give to you in heaven. WOW!!

I hope this has awakened your thinking to the tremendous purpose that God has for every Christian as long as they are living on this earth. This applies to every Christian living anywhere in the world and regardless of age. I encourage all of us to get busy about doing the work of God, and not wait on any kind of recognition from anyone on this earth.

9. What Crowns will Believers receive?

Whatever you do, work at it with all your heart, as working for the Lord, not for human masters, since you know that you will receive an inheritance from the Lord as a reward. It is the Lord Christ you are serving. Colossians 3:23-24

Everyone who competes in the games goes into strict training. They do it to get a crown that will not last, but we do it to get a crown that will last forever. 1 Corinthians 9:25

The Bible verses above encourage Believers to work with all their heart as if you were working for the Lord. I think this work includes everything you do: at a vocational job, at a church, as a member of a family, and as a Christian. It includes everything you do, and not just the church. The verses go on to say that you will receive an inheritance as a reward. The rewards that a Christian will receive from the Lord are called crowns.

Crowns are placed on the head of people to recognize them as royalty or as special people set apart from others. There are many crowns that the Bible says can be received by Believers.

Crown of Righteousness

I have fought the good fight, I have finished the race, I have kept the faith. Now there is in store for me the crown of righteousness, which the Lord, the righteous Judge, will award to me on that day—and not only to me, but also to all who have longed for his appearing. 2 Timothy 4:1-8

WOW!! Believers will receive a crown of righteousness. The qualifications to receive this crown are that you have fought many spiritual battles in your lifetime on earth. You faithfully put on the armor of God (see Ephesians 6), and waged war against all ungodliness in this world. You developed strong convictions about God's Word and His purpose for your life, and you would not allow anything to distract you from the goal of being Christ-like in all that you do. You maintained your faith during the hard times: financial, health, death of a loved one, etc. Finally, you lived your life on a daily basis as if Christ would return that day. You anticipated the Lord's Second Coming every day of your life.

Crown of Life

Blessed is the one who perseveres under trial because, having stood the test, that person will receive the crown of life that the Lord has promised to those who love him. James 1:12

The crown of Life is given to those Believers who persevere under trial. My first thought are all of the martyrs that have died in the name of Christ. They will receive this crown. For living Believers, there are trials that will test your faith. These trials can last a lifetime. They can be a heavy burden that Christians have to carry. The test is how does a Christian live through these burdens? Are they always complaining about their trial? Do they talk about themselves, and what they have to go through? Do they stop serving the Lord and others? This is a big one. Joni Erikson Tada is a beautiful example of a Believer who has had a lifetime trial and, yet, praises God every chance she gets. I do not doubt that she will receive the Crown of Life. How do you handle trials in your life...as a worldly person, or as a Believer in Christ?

Crown of Other Brothers and Sisters

Therefore, my brothers and sisters, you whom I love and long for, my joy and crown, stand firm in the Lord in this way, dear friends! Philippians 4:1

For what is our hope, our joy, or the crown in which we will glory in the presence of our Lord Jesus when he comes? Is it not you? Indeed, you are our glory and joy.

1 Thessalonians 2:19-20

This is a marvelous crown to receive from the Lord. This crown is given to those Believers who have had a part in leading a person to a point where they become a Christian. You can call this life-style evangelism. I know a woman who volunteered to lead a children's class on the spur of the moment. As she was going home after the class, she was almost in tears because she felt she did a horrible job with the kids. That afternoon, a mother of one of the children in her class called her and told her that he had accepted Christ because of what she had said. Glory to God! She will receive the crown of a Brother in Christ because she was a part of bringing someone to Christ. Are you actively involved in looking for opportunities that God has prepared for you to be a part of someone's salvation decision?

As a contrast to the Believers who are described above, there are some Believers who will not have strong convictions about Godly things, who will not stand strong during trials, and who will never tell anyone about their life with God.

But when you ask, you must believe and not doubt, because the one who doubts is like a wave of the sea, blown and tossed by the wind. That person should not expect to receive anything from the Lord. Such a person is double-minded and unstable in all they do. James 1:6-8

This is a tough contrast to the strongly convicted Believer, but it clearly says that a Believer who adapts his/her behavior to fit the situations in the world is considered unstable and double-minded. They will not receive anything from the Lord. I hope this helps you evaluate your Christians works through the Holy Spirit to determine what you do and why you do it.

There are other crowns in the Bible, but most of those are given to Believers who live during the Great Tribulation. Christ will give the three crowns discussed above to you, if you meet the qualifications of the work involved with each crown. I am not too sure that many Christians even think about what they are doing for God and the possibility of not receiving any crowns from Christ. You can start today by focusing on God's Kingdom on this earth. Its influence on this earth is directly related to the things you do as a Believer. Pray about your works by asking the Holy Spirit to make you more aware of what and why you do what you do for God. The results will have an eternal impact on other people's lives.

10. Death: The Last Enemy Christ Destroyed

Then the end will come, when he hands over the kingdom to God the Father after he has destroyed all dominion, authority and power. For he must reign until he has put all his enemies under his feet. The last enemy to be destroyed is death. 1 Corinthians 15:24-26

There have been a very few people in history who have tried to avoid death. All of them failed. All anyone can do is prolong the inevitable. You, me, and everyone you know will die. With the introduction of sin into our bodies, we will all eventually suffer physical death – separation from this earthly life. The verses above make it clear that Jesus Christ has defeated man's last enemy...death. As tough as this may sound, all Believers have an urgent need to understand, appreciate, and praise God for the significance of Christ defeating death. Let me give you a personal example.

When I was younger, I thought like most young people about death...I didn't! I had a life to live, and I wanted to live it to its maximum. Death is a "downer". It is depressing. I wanted to avoid the thoughts of my death as much as possible. What I did not realize was that death will always linger in the background of your life. This is why Jesus called " death" the last enemy to all Believers.

Death kept popping up when a loved one died, or when the news would announce someone's death. Movie stars and sports personalities seem to get an overdue amount of attention when they die. I have always wondered why? As human beings, we become interested when someone famous dies. However, their heart stops beating just exactly like your heart or my heart will stop beating. Every human being is on level ground when it comes to dying. Death is the one thing that none of us want to think about. UNLESS, you are a Believer! Death has been defeated by Christ to enable us to live eternally with God. It finally sunk into my thick skull that this is great news! This is difficult to say, but death is a time to celebrate for a Believer. We can now enter into the presence of the eternal God.

Death is a physical separation from the person who dies and those who remain living on this earth. There is always a time of adjustment when you lose a loved one. May I say that, as Believers, this adjustment time should become shorter and shorter? We should learn to vigorously celebrate the life of a Believer as a testimony to the supernatural work of the Holy Spirit. The Holy Spirit raised Jesus from the dead with an indestructible and glorified body. The Holy Spirit will do the same for each and every Believer. I suggest you read all of 1 Corinthians 15 to catch a glimpse of the "power" of your future resurrected body. You will come away impressed that God would make Believers " superhuman" (my term.) This is another appropriate time at the death of a Believer to praise God, show gratitude to Jesus Christ for defeating death, and look forward to the supernatural power of the Holy Spirit changing your old, weak, decaying body into a glorious, strong, never perishing resurrected body. Praise the Lord!

A Believer can truly ask death where is its victory and where is its sting. They do not exist because Jesus Christ has defeated death. Death is not a downer or a depressor for a Believer. Meditate on the following carefully: death has nothing but future hopes, spiritual peace, and physical healing for all Believers. The more I talk about death in this way, the more I want to join Paul in his desire to leave this world, and to go on to live with God. If all Believers would begin to encourage one another in this way, our perspective of death would be significantly different from the unbeliever. Do you think that God could use us in that situation as a living testimony to His unconditional love, forgiveness, and mercy? It is possible that someone may see God in you for the first time in their life and come to a personal intimate knowledge of who He is. Death has been nullified and removed as an emotional roller coaster for all Believers. Believers can now CELEBRATE the death of a Believer!

Let us all pray that we, as Believers, will not act as unbelievers when a loved one dies. Let us all be encouraged that our loved one, who is now with God, is experiencing no pain, has no tears in their eyes, gets a blinding smile on their face when they see Jesus, and will be able to move their bodies like no one on earth can through the supernatural power of the Holy Spirit. I hope you can demonstrate gratitude for Jesus defeating death. It may take you some time to renew your mind concerning the event called death, but DO IT!

11. Death: A Believer has nothing to fear

When the perishable has been clothed with the imperishable, and the mortal with immortality, then the saying that is written will come true: "Death has been swallowed up in victory." 1 Corinthians 15:53-55

Then death and Hades were thrown into the lake of fire. The lake of fire is the second death. Revelation 20:14

These are very comforting words if you believe them. God has taken the negative aspects of death for a Believer and turned them into positives. When we die, Believers enter the Presence of Christ. Death is a nothing to a Believer. At the end times, God will remove death from the presence of all Believers. He will throw it into the lake of fire that represents an eternal separation from God and His Kingdom.

God's Word says that when Christ was raised from the dead, he overcame death. Death was not more powerful than the Holy Spirit who raised Jesus from the dead. As a Believer, you have the same power residing in you. God has given you the power through the Holy Spirit to have already overcome death. Death has no claim on you. There is no reason to fear dying on this earth as a Believer. When you die, you will experience the identical resurrection as Jesus Christ! Do you believe this?

When death of a Believer occurs, I do not know how that makes you feel, but anything less than a celebration is not recognizing the greatly improved life of the one who died. You do not believe the Word of God. If you have a problem with this statement, then I suggest you spend more time thinking of heaven and not earth. The one who has died can see us and would love to tell us how great everything is. There is a purpose that God has for creating everything – He wants a strong, loving, intimate, and growing relationship with each one of us. That relationship becomes an ultimate reality when you die.

Satan has misused and abused death so that he can put fear into Believers. This fear is Biblically unfounded. Nothing in the Bible points to Christians as having the fear of dying. For some reason or other, a lot of us Believers believe the lie of Satan that, on this world, it "doesn't get any better than this." What a rotten, low-down, stinking lie. What is worse is that we will base the way we live on that lie. One of the most deceitful lies that Satan will tell a person who has lost a close loved one is "look at what you are going to miss about that person." There is no basis for fear of death in a Believer's life, either for themselves or a loved one.

Don't misunderstand what I am trying to say. Remembering a lost loved one is one of God's ways of ministering to you. He wants you to remember that person and all of the good times spent together. But, I think this "remembrance" is to increase your thoughts of heaven and the reunion that will occur when you die. It is not to look at the things that had yet to happen to that person here on this earth and you missed them. It is at times like these that you think more of yourself (selfishness) instead of your loved one seeing Jesus Christ every eternal day of their life.

Also, Satan would rather have you think of all the things that you are going to miss about this life. The world is not my choice for where I would like to spend eternity with my family. People who go on to heaven before us would love to tell us that. The way we live our lives on earth after the death of a loved one should be based on longing to be with them in heaven. This means that we look forward to our death instead of having an irrational fear of death.

God has purposed for you to remain on earth to continue to be a witness for Him. I cannot tell you what an awesome responsibility you have to testify about when you die, there will be angels singing in heaven and, hopefully, your loved ones on earth will be celebrating your new eternal life with Christ. I'm getting so excited about seeing my loved ones in heaven that if I keep writing, I'm going to ask God to go ahead and take me. But, He has work for me to do; so, in this world I must remain.

Similarly, God has things for you to do. Do not allow the fear of death to obtain a foothold in your life. Fear about death doesn't exist. It's a lie from Satan. God has taken care of death and has made it one on the greatest events in the life of a Believer. This is your testimony about a loving and all-powerful God.

Conclusion

1. God provides fruit of the Holy Spirit resulting from renewing of the mind

But the fruit of the Spirit is love, joy, peace, forbearance, kindness, goodness, faithfulness, gentleness and self-control. Against such things there is no law. Galatians 5:22-23

I love these verses. When the world has me tied up in knots...when my insides are like a washing machine or a cement mixer...when all I have heard from others are negative thoughts...when the news (CONTINUES) to be bad and is getting worse...when I feel so beat up on the inside...when all these things and more seem to be attacking me right and left with no end in sight, I need something to change my perspective. These verses change my perspective, and I hope they will yours.

The above verse is very clear on what that fruit of the Holy Spirit is: love, joy, peace, forbearance, kindness, goodness, faithfulness, gentleness, and self-control. I began to meditate on each one for a few minutes and my emotions seemed to be less significant in how I felt. With this testimony in mind, there are three things that I hope you come away with from reading this book.

1. A Believer saw another Believer hurting and was led by the Spirit to minister to that person. This is the Body of Christ that makes up the Kingdom of God on this earth. Too many of us Believers live in the Kingdom of this earth and never think that we do not belong to this earthly kingdom. We belong to the Kingdom of God, and we should

know how to act in that Kingdom. Helping a Believer to stay on course with the life purpose God has for them is every other Believer's responsibility for that Believer. Helping others when they are hurting is the responsibility of every other Believer. I hope you see that your sensitivity toward other Believers should actually be at a high level of awareness.

2. Fruit is the end product of the growth process of a live plant or tree. Fruit in the verses above are the results of Believers obeying God and following the Holy Spirit. This kind of fruit cannot be grown or produced by the flesh in any Believer. I would call that kind of fruit as "bad fruit", and all it is good for is to be fed to the hogs. I want to make this extremely clear to every Believer. The only good fruit is the fruit produced by the working of the Holy Spirit in their lives.

3. Finally, there is such a contrast between the fruit of the Spirit and the fruit of this world. For example, love – hate; joy – sadness; peace – fighting; forbearance (patience)–impatient; kindness – meanness; goodness – evil; faithfulness – untrustworthy; gentleness – harsh; and, self-control – flesh-control. If you can expose yourself to an environment that has the fruit of the Spirit, you will experience a life that is free and abundant. BUT, expose yourself to an environment that exhibits the opposite of the fruit of the Spirit, and you tell me what your attitude toward others, and your treatment toward others is like. It is like the kingdom of this earth.

Choose today to dwell on the fruit of the Spirit. Watch for fruit to be produced in other Believers and what caused the fruit to be produced. Let the Holy Spirit be your Counselor on how you react to the people in this world.

2. God[1]s purpose should always be on our minds

Therefore, my dear friends, as you have always obeyed—not only in my presence, but now much more in my absence—continue to work out your salvation with fear and trembling, for it is God who works in you to will and to act in order to fulfill his good purpose. Philippians 2:12-13

This is a clear statement concerning the work of Believers after accepting Christ. Many times I have read these verses and the wording, "work out your salvation" would cause me to stop and wonder how does work become part of our salvation.

Most Christians know that their salvation is not based on their works. You only receive salvation through the death of Christ on the cross. Jesus took His blood shed on the cross to the perfect altar that is in heaven. He spread His blood on that altar just like the Old Testament practice of spreading the blood of an unblemished lamb on the earthly altar located in the Temple. When Jesus presented His blood, salvation was now available to anyone who believes that Jesus took on the judgment from God for all of our sins. (See Hebrews, Chapter 9:16-28)

The Bible is clear in numerous places that human beings cannot receive salvation through their own efforts. This is stating the controversial issue of "faith versus works". It is a common misconception that human beings must do something to earn their salvation. Probably the most common "work" is to confess your sins. The Bible verse from 1 John 1:9 is the basis for this belief. However, the Greek word that is translated "to confess" actually has a more accurate interpretation as "to agree with". In other words, God wants you to agree with Him that you have sinned. Also, the verse is not discussing salvation. It is referring to the situation where you want to restore your relationship with God – not start your relationship.

The other interesting aspect of your salvation is that it will take place in the future. I would agree with you if you said, "I have salvation now." However, you receive your salvation from God when you die. As a result, God does not see you as a sinner, because the blood of Christ has covered over all of your sins. This enables you to live a holy eternal life before a Holy God while on this earth, and He expects that.

What is this work referring to? This is what you do while you remain on earth for God and for others. Basically, it is you allowing the Holy Spirit to guide you into random acts of kindness. You seek to put God's Kingdom into your life as a number one priority. You listen and prepare yourself to know God's will in all aspects of your life. This is working out your salvation.

The "fear and trembling" is not frequently associated with Christian work. However, it is time that Christians view this from God's perspective. He expects you to be His "slave". Before salvation, you were a slave to sin and free from God. As a Believer, you are now a slave to God and free from sin. See Romans, Chapter 6.

God wants to work in your life 24x7 so that His purpose is carried out on this earth. That purpose is for everyone to receive Christ as his or her Lord and Savior. God works in us in many and varied ways for this purpose to occur. As Christians, this spiritual purpose of God is why we should be practicing unconditional love for others, and always be ready to share what God has done in our lives. We are the only instruments that God has to carry out this purpose. It should always be on our minds at a high priority that we are here to do God's work.

3. Do you live in the darkness or the light?

"Arise, shine, for your light has come, and the glory of the Lord rises upon you. See, darkness covers the earth and thick darkness is over the peoples, but the Lord rises upon you. Nations will come to your light, and kings to the brightness of your dawn." Isaiah 60:1-3

You have probably heard several sermons on Believers being the "light of the world". You are the "light" that someone needs to see. The Light has come to you in the form of a Creator who has created and sustains everything, in the form of a baby in the manger, in the form of a Savior who has made a way for you to have a personal relationship with God. This Light has enveloped you so that others may see what they cannot see even with all the lights in the world. This Light is LIFE as God originally intended for every man, woman, and child.

"The glory of the Lord" is usually described as bright white light. I believe this glory is what surrounded Adam and Eve in the Garden before they sinned. When they sinned the glory left them. They could see each other's nakedness with lust in their heart. They realized that their impurity separated them from a holy God. This is why they hid. They did not want the light of God to reveal their disobedience. Their sin is the darkness that is spoken of in the verses above.

Darkness covers the earth. There are more people living a life for themselves than for God. A life lived like this is "thick darkness". I am including myself as well as many Christians in this condemnation. Today's Believers are not living the life that God intended. The world is full of darkness. It is interesting that most of the thick darkness occurs on earth at night and in dark places. There is a spiritual truth that, just like Adam and Eve, sinful man wants to hide from God. But God never runs out of grace for there is a great hope that God has for you as a Believer..."the Lord rises upon you."

God wants you to see that His glory is slowly enveloping you. As you live your life on this earth as a Christian, the Holy Spirit will lead you to make changes in your life that will reflect Jesus Christ...who is the Light of the world. Every change you make will increase the glory around you. This Light is Joy. This Light is Peace. This Light is Truth. This spiritual truth is confirmed in the New Testament:

> **And we, who with unveiled faces all reflect the Lord's glory, are being transformed into his likeness with ever increasing glory, which comes from the Lord, who is the Spirit.** 2 Corinthians 3:8

This is a tremendous spiritual truth that I hope sinks deep into your mind. This is God's purpose for your life. I strongly recommend that this truth be a part of your daily living. Consider that every day you live, God is putting people, incidents, and interactions into your life that are intended for you to lose some of your "darkness" and to gain some of God's glory ("light"). I had chills while I was writing this, because this is such a direct interaction between you and the Lord, who is the Spirit.

Lastly, you need to realize that, as you grow to be more Christ-like, you will expose the darkness of this world and that involves people. Do not expect to be welcomed by the darkness that covers other people (family members, friends, etc.) The darkness hates the light. The lust and greed in this world wants to be protected for what it proclaims, "Become rich, live in a luxurious house, drive an expensive car, and have anything you want that will make you happy."

Being happy in the darkness is not much fun, because the darkness will never allow you to become content with what you have. You will always want more and more until you are no longer the unique, special person that God created. You have become part of the masses in the thick darkness. All you can see is a mass of people moving around in the darkness not knowing where to go and always bumping into one another. Darkness is not a "happy place." I don't know why any Believer would want to continue to live in the darkness. Get out of the thick darkness now while the Holy Spirit is leading you!

Be prepared to give a reason for the Light that has arisen in you because of whom you trust and believe, the Lord and Savior, Jesus Christ. People will come to your light of life, joy, peace, and truth. They will want to leave the darkness when they see the glory of the Lord surrounding you.

4. Relationship with God must be a priority

And God spoke all these words: "I am the LORD your God, who brought you out of Egypt, out of the land of slavery. "You shall have no other gods before me.

"You shall not make for yourself an image in the form of anything in heaven above or on the earth beneath or in the waters below. You shall not bow down to them or worship them; for I, the LORD your God, am a jealous God. Exodus 20:1-5

All activities, works, thoughts, and plans of God are to achieve one purpose and only one purpose: have a strong and healthy relationship with you as a Believer. Most of you will recognize the above passage from Exodus that identifies the 10 Commandments. These are the first two commandments. They describe God's expectations of a relationship with every man, woman, and child. The setting is at Mt. Sinai where all of the Hebrews that Moses led out of Egypt were camped. They spent about two years at Mt. Sinai to learn more about God. It had been 400 years since God had any direct dealings with the Hebrews until He empowered Moses to deliver them from slavery.

The first statement is, "I am the LORD your God," like God introducing Himself to the people. The proper name for God is YHWH. The Hebrew language does not contain any vowels. The correct pronunciation has been lost because the Hebrews thought that no one was righteous enough to speak His name aloud. We pronounce it as "Yahweh". To know when the original Hebrew used the proper name for God "YHWH", modern translators used a technique of capitalizing all the letters of LORD, but reducing the font size of the three last characters. Therefore, when you see in your Bibles, LORD, you know that it is referring to the proper name of God. This becomes extremely important to know when God is being referred to.

The remaining passage describes God's expectations of your relationship with Him. It says that you should have no other gods in your life. Something in this world can become a god to you when you devote time to it ahead of everything else. My career was a god to me for the first seven years of employment. I did not think of other things in my life other than my job. I look back on those seven years with a harsh judgment of myself, because I had a beautiful and devoted wife and two unbelievable children. I wish I had not missed their early lives, but it is too late. This is what another god will do to you. You will miss the important things in your life.

God continues to explain His expectations of a relationship with you when He says that you should not make an image that you will worship. For many men, a car can easily become an image that is worshipped by them. For women, it could be certain cosmetics or a TV talk show that takes precedence over other things in their lives.

Finally, God says He is a jealous God. He doesn't want to share you with anyone or anything else. Your relationship to Him should be first in your life. This relationship between you and God takes work just like with any other relationship. The depth and strength of your relationship with God is determined by the amount of time spent together and talking about things. This is God's desire: a working, talking, and living relationship with you. Let Him know how you feel about things. Listen to Him through the Holy Spirit. Your life will be different with a strong relationship with God.

5. Going God's way will make your life fulfilled

As for God, his way is perfect; the word of the LORD is flawless. He is a shield for all who take refuge in him. For who is God besides the LORD? And who is the Rock except our God? It is God who arms me with strength and makes my way perfect. Psalm 18:30-32

One thing you can learn from the verses above is that God's way is perfect. What does "his way" mean? Think a moment about the "way" you live. How do you make decisions? How do you handle problems and setbacks? How do you treat others? What do you do in your spare time? If I could observe you in these situations, I would have a good idea about the "way" you live your life.

God is saying that his "way" is perfect. There are no imperfections in His creating and sustaining everything. Your way is not perfect, because you are a sinner and the flesh desires to control you. You may have good intentions, but they are slowly forgotten if your expectations are not met. The "way" of God is through Jesus Christ. Jesus revealed God to us. We know God from learning about Christ. Jesus said that He was the Way, the Truth, and the Life.

His Word is flawless. You can read the Bible knowing that it has been scrutinized more than any other book and continues to pass the test of "without error in giving hope to people." There is nothing in this world that you can put your faith in that will not eventually fail you (including people – parents, siblings, husband/wife.) We all fail someone in some way. I take great comfort in reading the Bible, because it is solid and without any errors. Reason may plant the suggestion of errors in the Bible resulting in doubts about God's existence and His power to overcome all things. If this is you, I wish you the best in what this world will do to you. Faith in a flawless Bible frees you to have God reveal Himself to you, resulting in a fulfilled, purposeful, and abundant life.

God is also a shield for you. When life throws things at you, God protects you, and you may never be aware of it. Now, some people like to have things thrown at them because of their egos ("I can do it myself!"), or because they want others to feel sorry for what they "have" to go through in life. The secure Believer is depending solely on God as a shield. It's not about the "me"; it's all about Him.

When you are settled in your mind about God's way, His Word, and that He protects you, then you are free to develop wholesome relationships with others. This is God's purpose in giving you His way, Word, and protection. Only when you know that you have those things will you open up to others. You will not have a problem in being transparent to others. The opposite of being transparent is being hypocritical. We have too much hypocrisy in our churches, because we do not rely on God's Way, His Word, and His Protection.

6. Praise and worship to a God who never changes

"Blessed be your glorious name, and may it be exalted above all blessing and praise. You alone are the Lord. You made the heavens, even the highest heavens, and all their starry host, the earth and all that is on it, the seas and all that is in them. You give life to everything, and the multitudes of heaven worship you. Nehemiah 9:5-6

They refused to listen and failed to remember the miracles that you performed among them. They became stiff-necked and in their rebellion appointed a leader in order to return to their slavery. But you are a forgiving God, gracious and compassionate, slow to anger and abounding in love. Therefore you did not desert them. Nehemiah 9:17

These two passages are from the book of Nehemiah. This is one of the last books in the chronology of events in the Old Testament. All of Israel had been dispersed by Assyria and Babylon. The Temple and the walls of Jerusalem had been destroyed. The Temple was rebuilt first, but the people grew tired and complacent in rebuilding the walls for protection. Nehemiah had come from Babylon to encourage the people to rebuild the walls. The walls were completed around 445BC. After the walls were rebuilt, Ezra led a great revival of the reading of the Word of God. The people stood for days listening to Ezra read. Eventually, the people recognized their sins against God. I share this passage with you to help you in your praise of God.

They first lifted the name of God above everything that existed and everything that they knew: "may your name be exalted above all blessing and praise." There are many names used to refer to God in the Old Testament. Make it a goal that you will learn some of the names of God and what they mean.

The priests spoke of God's Creation and its completeness. They included everything that they could physically see: "you made the heavens, even the highest heavens and all their starry host." This is interesting because it implies that there are many heavens. Spiritually speaking, we are very ignorant of all of space and the spiritual realms. There is much more than we can see. God created the earth and all that is in it. God gives life to everything meaning that all of life is in the hands of God. This is why it is so meaningful to realize that Jesus defeated death and was resurrected, as all Believers will experience. It is for this reason that death has no hold on Believers, and we do not fear death. The final statement in the first passage references all the multitudes of the heaven as worshipping God. This is what we should think on when we are praising God.

I included the last passage as a rebuttal to those who believe that the God of the Old Testament was a harsh, wrathful, judgmental, and different from the God is love in the New Testament. The passage clearly describes the forgiveness of God. It describes the grace and compassion of God toward the people who were repeatedly disobedient to Him. Finally, it describes His patience (slow to anger) and His love. I do not know how anyone can conclude that there are two different Gods in the Old and New Testament. He is the same yesterday, today, and tomorrow. Praise His name above everything that you and I know.

My last thought for you is to begin journaling about your spiritual life. I did several years of journaling that proved to be extremely beneficial. I grew in my discussions with God. I could see how he had worked in my life in my earlier years to put me in places that I found myself. My relationships with others (especially, with my wife and children) became more enriching. It was easier to see their needs and minister to them as a Husband and father. I was able to keep my priorities with God without compromise.

If you journal over several years, you will see how your mind went through a process of transformation. This is the main reason that I wrote this book. The renewal of the mind is God's priority for every Believer. To make it part of your spiritual life is the most effective way that you will grow to become more Christ-like.

About the Author

I, Carlton Lee Arnold, experienced a spiritual awakening at the age of 30. Simply put, God told me that life was to be centered either on God or on me. I experienced the love of God that resulted in my salvation when I was 12. God continued to work on my life through numerous secular jobs. I served in the U.S. Air Force for seven years. My early career in computers established a strong path of various computer and network jobs. I retired in 2003 after holding several management positions in the Information Technology industry. God designed all of my secular jobs for me to obtain a broad knowledge of people and people skills.

At 30 years of age, God gave me a heart for His Word that has never left me. For the past 38 years, constant reading and studying His Word has permitted me to teach Bible classes and write several books. I have no formal religious education. Everything that comes from me is a direct result of the leadership of the Holy Spirit.

God has been especially gracious to enable me to help others to understand the Bible from their point of view. One of the major aspects that God has enabled for me to accomplish is to present the Bible from a single spiritual perspective. Many people have spiritually benefitted from this ability.

While working as Director of Adult Discipleship at First Baptist Cumming, GA, I began to write weekly articles of encouragement. This led me to write several books that are mentioned below. To find out more, go to www.lifechangingverses.com. You will find Video lessons and written commentaries about the Old and New Testaments. You will also find a weekly article that I have published for the past seven years. Comments and interviews from radio and TV are also contained on the web site. Finally, a description of the books published by me can be found there.

Other books published by the Author:

These books are available through most online bookstores. You can also order the books through your local bookstore. Note: Local walk-in bookstores do not stock books that are written by self-published authors. You can request that the book be ordered.

Life-Changing Verses, Volume 1

Life-Changing Verses, Volume 2

Life-Changing Verses, Volume 3

God and Men: No-Holds Barred

A Huge Thank You!

I deeply appreciate my wife, D'Ette, for her help in getting this book published. Her editing skills were invaluable. Our joint discussions over several topics contained in this book helped me stay on track with a clear mind. On June 10, 2019, we will celebrate 50 years of marriage. We have truly become one before God in all that we do.

We have two fantastic children, Eric and Erin. God richly blessed us with wonderful mates for both of our children. Eric's wife Ginger and Erin's husband, Joey makes the family complete. We also have three beautiful and intelligent grandchildren: Garrett, McKenna, and Ella.

Our lives are not complete and are very dull without our family. We love all of them greatly.

CPSIA information can be obtained
at www.ICGtesting.com
Printed in the USA
LVOW08s1619031116
511532LV00010B/925/P